For

Teagan Aryanna Lowery
on the occasion of
your dedication
to the LORD.

May Jesus light your way
every day of your life.

Love,
Omi and Papi

Jesus Loves Me
BIBLE
STORYBOOK &
DEVOTIONAL

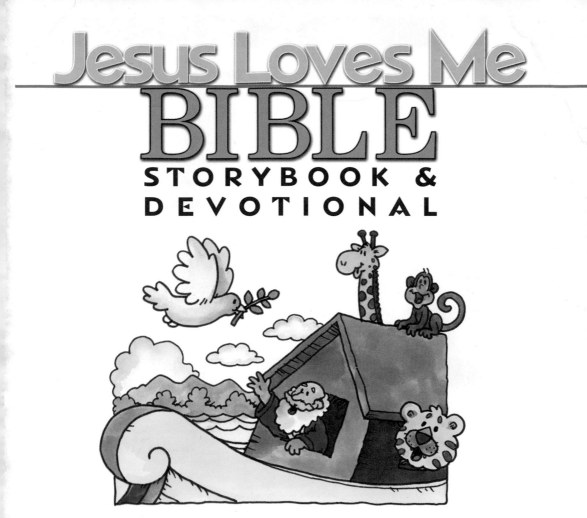

Stories retold by **Angela Abraham and Ken Abraham**

Illustrations by **Terry Anderson and Kathleen Dunne**

Concept by **Michael and Dorene Briggs**

Tommy NELSON®

www.tommynelson.com

A Division of Thomas Nelson, Inc.
www.ThomasNelson.com

The *Jesus Loves Me Bible Storybook & Devotional* is designed to be an all-in-one resource for sharing faith with your child. The Bible storybook is comprised of 120 stories from the Old and New Testaments. It is written especially for the young child, with clear, simple text and colorful illustrations. The devotional pairs stories of favorite Bible characters with songs, prayers, simple projects, and small challenges in order to guide children in applying God's Word to their daily lives. The index in the back of the devotional is cross-referenced with the Bible storybook to provide more background on the theme of each day's devotional. Whether you're looking for an interactive devotional or an entertaining Bible story, you'll find everything you need in this one book.

JESUS LOVES ME BIBLE STORYBOOK & DEVOTIONAL

This book was written by Angela Abraham and Ken Abraham. Angela is a freelance writer and was formerly a children's church coordinator for Christ Church in Nashville, Tennessee. Ken is the author of more than twenty books. Illustrations are by Terry Anderson and Kathleen Dunne through Rosenthal Represents, Los Angeles, California.

JESUS LOVES ME BIBLE (formerly titled THE HOSANNA BIBLE)
Text copyright © 1993, 1999 by Angela Abraham and Ken Abraham.
Art copyright © 1993, 1999 by Tommy Nelson®, a Division of Thomas Nelson, Inc.

JESUS LOVES ME DEVOTIONAL (formerly titled PRAISE AND WORSHIP: A Devotional for Little Ones)
Text copyright © 1996, 1999 by Angela Abraham and Ken Abraham.
Art copyright © 1996, 1999 by Terry Anderson and Kathleen Dunne.

Published in Nashville, Tennessee, by Tommy Nelson®, a Division of Thomas Nelson, Inc.

Scripture quotations are from the International Children's Bible®, New Century Version®, © 1983, 1986, 1988, 1999, Tommy Nelson®, a Division of Thomas Nelson, Inc.

ISBN 1-4003-0185-8

Printed in Columbia

04 05 06 QWB 9 8 7 6 5

Jesus Loves Me
BIBLE
STORYBOOK

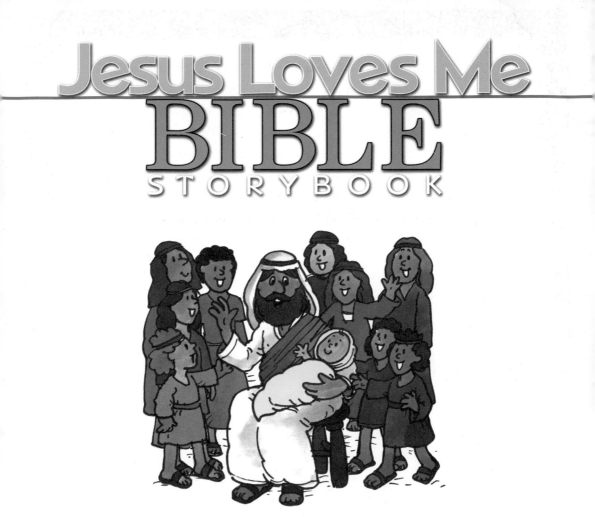

Stories *retold by* **Angela Abraham and Ken Abraham**

Illustrations by **Terry Anderson and Kathleen Dunne**

Concept by **Michael and Dorene Briggs**

Tommy NELSON

www.tommynelson.com

A Division of Thomas Nelson, Inc.
www.ThomasNelson.com

To Meaghan, Ashleigh,
Alyssa, and all their friends.
May the Lord's praises be
ever on your lips and
in your heart.

Contents

OLD TESTAMENT

NEW TESTAMENT

Old Testament

*"***I** am the Lord your God. You must be holy because I am holy."*

—Leviticus 19:2

GOD'S GARDEN

"In the beginning God created the sky and the earth." Genesis 1:1

Long ago, God made the world.
The earth was dark.
The sky was empty and black.
But God's Spirit looked over the world.
He had a wonderful plan!

When God spoke, the heavens appeared.
He blessed the earth with beauty.
God shaped the high mountains.
He filled the lakes with cool water.
He made the soft grass, fresh fruit, and bright
flowers that smell sweet.
God told the sun to shine in the day and the
stars to twinkle at night.

God made fish to splash and swim in the seas.
He made birds to sing and fly through
the air.
Then He filled the earth with animals:
Some that crawl and creep.
Some that jump and leap.
God said, "Let Us make someone to care for
My wonderful world!"

God molded a man from dirt and breathed
life into him.
He named the man Adam.
Then He formed a woman to help Adam.
Her name was Eve. God placed them in a
beautiful garden called Eden.
In six days, God made everything good.
On the seventh day, He rested from all His work.

THE FRUIT TREE

". . . In the middle of the garden, God put the tree that gives . . . the knowledge of good and evil." GENESIS 2:9

Adam and Eve were happy in their special garden home. They walked and talked with God. He was their friend.

God told them, "You may eat fruit from any tree, except one. If you eat from the tree in the middle of the garden, you will die!"

Adam and Eve obeyed God.

One day, something terrible happened.
A sneaky snake asked Eve, "Did God really
tell you not to eat any of this tasty fruit?"
Eve looked at the beautiful fruit in the middle
of the garden.
"Taste some," said the snake. "It will make
you wise like God. You won't die."

Satan used the snake to trick Eve.
She ate the forbidden fruit.
Then she took some to Adam, and he tasted it.
Suddenly, Adam and Eve heard God walking
in the garden.
They had disobeyed God, so they were afraid.
Where could they hide from God?

"Adam, Adam, where are you?" God called.
"Why are you hiding?"
Adam answered, "I heard Your voice, and I
was frightened."
"Did you eat the fruit I told you not to
touch?" God asked.
"The woman gave it to me!" said Adam.
"The snake said it was okay to eat!" said Eve.

God was sad that they had not obeyed Him.
God cursed the snake. "You will crawl on
your belly forever!"
God told Adam and Eve, "Because you chose
to sin, you must leave the garden."
Then He made animal clothing for them to
wear and sent them away from their lovely
garden home.

BLOOD BROTHERS

"If you do good, I will accept you. But if you do not do good, sin is ready to attack you. Sin wants you. But you must rule over it." GENESIS *4:7*

Adam and Eve had many children.
Their first sons were named Cain and Abel.
Cain was a farmer.
Abel took care of sheep.

One day Cain and Abel were worshiping
God. They each brought God a gift.
Abel's gift was good.
But Cain's gift was selfish.
Cain's gift did not please God.

Cain was angry that God did not accept his offering. Cain wanted to kill Abel.

"Your heart is angry," God said. "Do good and I will accept you." But Cain did not obey God.

Cain hit Abel and killed him.

"Where is your brother?" God asked.
Cain yelled, "I don't know. Is it my job to
take care of him?"
God said, "I see what you did to your brother.
You will be punished for the terrible way
you treated him."
God told Cain, "Your heart is evil. You
cannot stay in My presence."
Cain roamed the earth without God.

RAIN, RAIN, GO AWAY

"The Lord said, 'My Spirit will not remain in human beings forever. . . .'"
GENESIS 6:3

The earth was crowded with wicked people.
God was sorry that He made man.
He said, "I will destroy everything on earth
and start again!"
But God saw one good man who tried to
do right.

God told Noah, "I will drown the earth in a
flood of water. You will be saved, if you
build a big boat."
Noah did everything God said.
He built a boat tall and wide.
His family and many animals would hide
safely inside.

Noah put two of every kind of animal on the boat—alligators, elephants, monkeys, and bears; every animal pair marched onto the boat. And God shut the door tight.

Thunder and lightning crashed.
Rain poured from the sky.
It stormed for forty days and nights.
The water rose high above the mountain peaks.

Finally, God sent a wind to dry the earth.
And the boat touched solid ground.
Then Noah sent a dove from the boat.
The dove returned with an olive leaf in his
beak. And Noah knew that the ground was
almost dry.

When Noah left the boat, he built an altar.
He thanked God for saving his family.
God was very pleased. He blessed Noah.
God said, "I will never again destroy the
earth with a flood. A rainbow in the sky will
be the sign of My promise to you."

CHATTER SCATTER

"Then they said to each other, 'Let's build for ourselves a city and a tower. And let's make the top of the tower reach high into the sky. We will become famous. . . .'" GENESIS 11:4

Soon the earth was full of people again. Everyone used the same language to talk. The people said, "Let's build a city with a tall tower to show how wonderful we are." These proud people thought they were greater than God.

God was not happy. So he mixed up their speech. The people stopped building the tower and scattered to every land.
And the city was named *Babel*, which means "confusion." From then on, people living in different lands spoke their own languages.

GOD'S PROMISE

". . . The Lord said, 'I am God All-Powerful. Obey me and do what is right. I will make an agreement between us. I will make you the ancestor of many people.'" GENESIS 17:1, 2

Abram worshiped God.
His neighbors prayed to false gods.
God told Abram, "Leave this country.
Go to a new land, and I will bless you."
Abram obeyed God.

Abram packed all his things and moved.
Then God appeared to Abram,
"I will give to your family all the land you see."
Abram thanked God.

One night God spoke to Abram in a vision,
"Can you count the stars at night?
I will bless you with so many children,
you will not be able to count them."
Later God changed Abram's name to Abraham.
Again, God said, "You will be father of many."

Abraham was now ninety-nine years old.
God said, "Your wife, Sarah, will have a son."
Abraham said, "Sarah and I are too old to have children."
"Is anything too hard for the Lord?" said God.
Isaac was the son born to Sarah and Abraham.
Isaac means "laughter."

JEHOVAH-JIREH

"So Abraham named that place The Lord Gives. Even today people say, 'On the mountain of the Lord it will be given.'" Genesis 22:14

One day God tested Abraham's love.
He said, "Abraham, I want you to give up
your only son." He told Abraham to sacrifice
Isaac on an altar.
This was a terribly hard thing to do.
Abraham loved Isaac very much.
But Abraham also trusted God.

Early the next morning, Abraham took Isaac
to a mountain and built an altar.
Isaac said, "Father, where is the lamb for the
sacrifice?"
Abraham said, "God will take care of it."

Then Abraham laid his son on the altar.
Suddenly, the angel of God shouted,
"Abraham! Abraham! Do not hurt the boy.
Since you have obeyed Me, I now know that
you love God most."

Then Abraham saw a ram caught by his horns in the bushes. Abraham sacrificed the ram instead of his only son.

Abraham named that place *Jehovah-Jireh*, which means, "The Lord will provide."

God blessed Abraham with a great reward because he trusted the Lord.

A WIFE FOR LIFE

". . . 'The Lord will send his angel before you. The angel will help you get a wife for my son there.'" GENESIS 24:7

It was time for Isaac to find a wife.
The local girls worshiped false gods.
Abraham worried. His grandchildren might
become idol worshipers if Isaac married a
local girl.

Abraham said to his loyal servant, "Go to my homeland and bring back a wife for Isaac."
"How will I choose the girl?" the servant asked.
"The Lord will send His angel before you. He will help you," said Abraham.

The servant traveled to Abraham's old town.
He stopped by a well to pray,
"Lord, please lead me to the right girl."
The young girls from town were walking
toward the well. The servant prayed, "When
I ask for a drink, let the girl for Isaac
answer me."

Just then, a beautiful girl named Rebekah came to the well. She gave the servant a drink of water. She said, "I will get your camels a drink, too."

The servant praised God for answering his prayer. "God has been kind and truthful. Rebekah is the right wife for Isaac's life."

THE TWIN THAT WINS

"Esau said, 'Jacob is the right name for him. He has tricked me these two times. He took away my share of everything you own. And now he has taken away my blessing.'" GENESIS 27:36

After Abraham died, his son Isaac became the owner of all his tents, sheep, cattle, camels, and servants.
Now, Isaac and Rebekah had twin boys.
Esau was the oldest son.
He would receive more of his father's riches and God's promises.
Jacob was the younger brother.

One day, Esau came in from hunting.
Jacob was cooking some vegetable soup.
"Mmm, that soup smells good. I'm starved.
Let me have a bite!" said Esau.
"Sure, if you sell me your part of father's
wealth," said Jacob slyly.
Esau did not appreciate the promises of God.
He sold his future riches for a bowl of soup.

When Isaac was old and blind,
he called for Esau, "I want to give you God's
blessing before I die. Go hunting for an
animal that is good to eat. Then make me a
tasty meal. I will bless you after dinner."
Rebekah heard Isaac's words. She told Jacob
how to get the blessing Isaac was going to
give Esau.

Isaac could not see, so Jacob pretended to be
Esau. Jacob dressed like his brother and raced
to Isaac's tent.
"Is that really you, Esau? Come closer so I can
touch you," said Isaac. Jacob wore animal
skins to make his skin feel hairy like Esau's.
Jacob tricked Isaac into giving him the
blessing.

BETHEL, "GOD'S HOUSE"

"Then Jacob woke from his sleep. He said, 'Surely the Lord is in this place.'" GENESIS *28:16*

Esau hated Jacob for stealing his blessing.
Rebekah warned Jacob, "You must leave this
place before Esau tries to kill you. Go to your
grandfather's old home and hide."
Jacob started his long journey.
One night, he used a stone for a pillow.
In a dream he saw angels climbing up and
down a ladder to heaven.
God was standing above the ladder. He said,
"I will give you the land where you are
sleeping. And I will protect you everywhere
you go."

When Jacob woke up he said, "Surely the Lord is in this place." He named the place *Bethel*, which means "house of God."

A FIGHT AT NIGHT

"So Jacob named that place Peniel. He said, 'I have seen God face to face. But my life was saved.'" GENESIS *32:30*

Many years passed before Jacob went back home.
God had blessed him with great wealth.
He was married and had many children.
One day, he got news that Esau was nearby.
Esau had an army of men.
Jacob feared for his family's safety.

Jacob prayed, "Lord, You said You would watch over me! I am afraid Esau will kill us! Please, protect us."

Jacob prepared a very special gift of many animals for Esau.

Jacob thought, *"Esau might forgive me when he sees this gift."*

That night, Jacob prayed again.
A man wrestled with him until morning.
Jacob's leg was hurt, but he would not stop
struggling.
"You can't go until you bless me," said Jacob.
The man said, "Your name will be changed
from Jacob to Israel. For you have wrestled
with God and won the victory!"

Later, Jacob saw Esau.
Jacob bowed low before him.
Esau had forgiven his brother.
He ran to Jacob and kissed him.
The brothers cried. They were happy to see
each other.

THE SLAVE WHO FORGAVE

"Then Joseph said to them, 'Don't be afraid. . . . You meant to hurt me. But God turned your evil into good. . . . I will take care of you and your children. . . .'" GENESIS 50:19–21

Jacob lived in the land of Canaan with his
twelve sons. Joseph was his favorite son.
Jacob made Joseph a colorful coat.
All the brothers were jealous.
When Joseph had a strange dream, his
brothers hated him even more.

"Brothers, listen to my dream," Joseph said proudly. "We were in the field tying bundles of wheat. My bundle of wheat stood up. Your bundles bowed down to mine."

"Do you want to be our king?" Joseph's brothers asked angrily.

Before long, Joseph dreamed again that his family would bow down to him.

One day, Joseph's brothers grabbed him.
They tore off his bright coat and threw him
in a pit. Then a group of traders passed by.
"Let's sell Joseph to the traders," the brothers
agreed. They sold him for twenty pieces of
silver.
The traders took Joseph to Egypt and sold
him as a slave.

Joseph worked hard in Egypt.
God blessed everything he did.
Soon, his master put him in charge of all the
master owned. Then the master's wife lied
about Joseph.
Joseph was thrown into prison, even though
he was not guilty. But God was with Joseph
there.

One night, the king of Egypt had two
dreams. No one in Egypt could explain the
meaning to him. Someone told the king that
Joseph could explain dreams. The king sent
for Joseph.
When Joseph heard the dreams, he told the
king that God was warning him.
"There will be seven years of plenty in Egypt,
followed by seven years of hunger," Joseph
said.

"We should store up food during the years of
plenty. Then everyone will have enough food
during the famine."

The king said, "Joseph, you are filled with the
spirit of God, and you are wise. I want you to
be in charge of the food project."

The king gave Joseph the highest position in
the land, next to the king.

Everything that Joseph said would happen came true. Egypt was the only land that saved food for the famine years. Hungry people came from every country to Egypt. One day, Joseph's brothers came all the way from Canaan to buy food.

They did not know they would have to buy
their food from Joseph.
All the brothers bowed down before the
governor of Egypt.
They did not know he was Joseph.

Joseph recognized his brothers. But he kept
quiet until they visited again.
"Brothers, it is I, Joseph," he finally said.
"Don't be afraid of me. God turned into good
what you meant to be evil."

Joseph told his brothers to move to Egypt so
they would have plenty to eat.
Jacob was happy when he heard that Joseph
was alive. He built an altar to thank God.
At last Jacob's family reached Egypt. Joseph
came in his chariot to meet them. He couldn't
wait to see his father.

BABY IN A BASKET

"'I am . . . the God of your father. Don't be afraid to go to Egypt. I will make your descendants a great nation there. . . . And I will bring you out of Egypt again.'" GENESIS *46:3, 4*

At first, the children of Jacob were treated well in Egypt. The family grew larger, and they were called Israelites.

Many years passed.

There was a new king in Egypt.

He did not know Joseph or the wonderful way he had saved the hungry people.

He feared the Israelites would soon out-
number his own people.
So, he made them his slaves.
He made them work hard.
Still, the children of Israel grew in numbers.
To stop this, the evil king decided to kill all of
the Israelite baby boys.

A mother hid her baby in a basket by the river. One day, the king's daughter came to the river to bathe. She found the baby in the basket. The baby started to cry, and she felt sorry for him. She adopted the baby as her own son and named him Moses.

Moses grew up as a prince in the palace.
Meanwhile, God's people suffered as slaves.
One day, Moses saw an Egyptian man
beating an Israelite slave.
Moses killed the Egyptian.
When the king found out, he wanted to kill
Moses. But Moses ran away to hide in the
desert.

A SPECIAL STICK

"Then God said to Moses, 'I AM WHO I AM.' When you go to the people of Israel, tell them, 'I AM has sent me to you.'" EXODUS 3:14

One day, Moses saw a burning bush that did not burn up.
God called to Moses from the bush, "Moses! Moses! Take off your shoes. Do not come any closer to Me. You are standing on holy ground."
Moses covered his face. He was afraid.

The Lord said, "I have heard the prayers of My people. Go tell the king to free My people so they can worship Me. I want you to lead My people out of Egypt."

Moses said, "I'm not a great man. What if the people of Israel do not want me for their leader?"

God said, "Tell them *Yahweh* sent you. I AM WHO I AM."

The Lord told Moses to throw down his walking stick. Moses did. And the stick changed into a hissing snake.

God said, "Grab the snake by its tail." Moses was afraid, but he obeyed God. The snake turned back into a stick.

God said, "Show My people this miracle. They will know *Yahweh* has sent you."

BOILS AND BUGS

*"Moses said to the Lord, 'But Lord, I am not a skilled speaker. . . .'
Then the Lord said to him, 'Who made man's mouth? . . . Now
go! I will tell you what to say.'"* EXODUS *4:10, 11, 12*

Moses told God, "I'm not a good speaker."
God said, "Your brother Aaron will speak
for you."
Aaron and Moses went to see the king of
Egypt. They said, "God wants you to let His
people go!"
The king said angrily, "I don't know your God."
The mean king made the Israelite slaves work
even harder.

Moses was discouraged.

God told him, "I am the Lord, God All-Powerful.

Now you will see what I will do to the king."

God turned all the water in Egypt to blood.

The Egyptians had no water to drink.

The Israelites' water stayed pure.

But the king would not let God's people go.

Aaron raised the special stick over all the
waters of Egypt, and the land was filled with
frogs. The king said to Moses, "Ask your God to
take the frogs away. I will let your people go."
Then Moses prayed, and God removed the frogs.
But the king broke his promise. He would not
let God's people go.

God punished Egypt with terrible plagues.
He covered their land with bugs. He caused
their animals to die. Both people and
animals got horrible sores. The crops were
killed in a hail storm. Then locusts ate all the
plants the storm didn't kill.
Finally, it was dark in Egypt for three days.
Still, the stubborn king refused to listen to God.

Moses went to see the king one last time.
Moses said, "Tonight, every firstborn son in
Egypt will die. But the Israelites will be
unharmed."
The king did not listen. He yelled, "Get out
of here, or I will kill you!"

THE CHOSEN PEOPLE

"When I see the blood, I will pass over you. . . . You are always to remember this day. Celebrate it with a feast to the Lord. . . ."
Exodus *12:13, 14*

The Lord told the Israelites what to do to get ready for "the Passover."
Each family cooked a lamb for a special meal. They wiped the lamb's blood on the sides and top of their door frames.
That night, every firstborn son of the Egyptians died. But God protected the Israelites. He passed over every home that had blood on the door frame.

During the night, the king called for Moses.
He said, "Take your people out of this land.
Go worship your God."
The Egyptian people gave their jewelry and
riches to the Israelites.
The Egyptians were afraid of Israel's God.
All the Israelites quickly packed and left
Egypt together.

THROUGH THE SEA

" ' I will sing to the Lord because he is worthy of great honor. He has thrown the horse and its rider into the sea. The Lord gives me strength and makes me sing. He has saved me. He is my God, and I will praise him.'" EXODUS 15:1, 3

God led the people of Israel out of Egypt.
During the day, He traveled ahead of the Israelites in a great cloud.
At night, He was a pillar of fire, so they were not in darkness. The Lord God showed His children which way to go.
The Israelites followed the Lord's great cloud to the edge of the Red Sea.
When the king of Egypt realized he had let all his slaves go, he changed his mind.
He chased after the Israelites with his army.

The Israelites were terrified when they saw the king's chariots racing after them.

Moses said, "Don't be afraid! Stand still and watch the Lord fight for you!"

The Lord caused the water to separate. The Israelites crossed the sea on dry land.

The king's chariots chased after the children of Israel.

When the Israelites got to the other side, the water came back together. And the king's army drowned in the sea.

Then, Moses and the Israelites sang praises to the Lord. Moses' sister, Miriam, took a tambourine in her hand. All the women followed her, playing tambourines and dancing.

MEAT TO EAT

" ' You must obey the Lord, your God . . . and keep his rules. If you do these things, I will not give you any of the sicknesses I gave the Egyptians.' " EXODUS 15:26

The Israelites traveled through the desert for three days. They started complaining to Moses because they had no water. Then the water they found was bitter, so the Lord showed Moses a tree to put in the water to make it taste good.

God said, "You must obey Me. If you do, I will keep you well. I am the Lord who heals you."

Soon, the people began grumbling to Moses again. "We don't have any meat to eat," they said.

"In Egypt we had plenty of food. Are we going to starve in the desert?"

The Lord sent them quail and manna from heaven. The people had bread and meat to eat each day.

THE LORD IS MY BANNER

*"Then Moses built an altar. He named it THE LORD IS MY BANNER.
Moses said, 'I lifted my hands toward the Lord's throne.'"*
EXODUS *17:15, 16*

The Israelites stopped to rest in the desert.
Suddenly, wild people who lived in the hills
attacked them. Moses quickly called out all
the men who were prepared to fight.
He made Joshua their leader.
The Israelites went to war against the wild
people. Moses raised his hands toward
heaven. He prayed for God to help His
people.

When Moses' hands were lifted up, the Israelites won. When Moses got tired, he let his arms drop down. And the enemy started to win. Two men stood beside Moses. They held his hands high until God's children won the battle. Then Moses called the place *Jehovah-Nissi* which means, "The Lord Is My Banner."

HOLY GROUND

" 'You must worship the Lord your God. If you do, I will bless your bread and your water. I will take away sickness from you. . . . I will allow you to live long lives.' " EXODUS 23:25, 26

Finally, the Israelites reached the Sinai Mountain. This was the place where God had spoken to Moses from the burning bush. The Lord called Moses to the mountain. He said, "Tell the people they must wash their clothes. They must prepare themselves for service to God. Then, I will come down on the mountain."

The Lord warned Moses, "Do not let the people touch the mountain. This is a holy place where I will show My glory."
Three days later, the people heard a loud trumpet blast and thunder. They saw fire and lightning. A thick cloud covered the mountain. The people were frightened. They heard the voice of God speak to Moses.

God called Moses to the mountain top.
God said, "I am the Lord your God.
I brought you out of slavery in Egypt."
Then God gave ten rules to help His people
live right. He wrote them on stone tablets.

*I am the only, one true God. Love and
    worship Me.*
Do not worship or serve any other god.
Do not curse or swear using God's name.
Rest on the Sabbath day; keep it holy.
Honor your father and mother.
Do not kill people.
Husbands and wives be faithful to each other.
Do not steal.
Do not lie.
*Do not wish for things that belong to someone
    else.*

God told Moses, "I've written My rules.
Now you can teach them to the people."

A GOLDEN CALF

"And the Lord said to Moses, '. . . They have quickly turned away from the things I commanded them to do.'" EXODUS 32:7–8

Moses stayed on the mountain forty days. The people thought he wasn't coming back. They no longer feared the Lord's presence nor kept His rules.

One day the people said to Aaron, "Make us
a god we can see."
He melted their gold jewelry and molded it
into the shape of a calf.
The people bowed down to worship it.

The Lord told Moses, "Hurry down the mountain. The people are worshiping another god. They have made Me angry. Now, I will destroy them!"

"Lord, please forget Your anger," Moses begged. "Remember Your promises to us." The Lord listened to Moses and did not destroy the Israelites.

Moses returned to the Israelite camp.
He found the wicked people dancing around
the golden calf. Moses smashed the stone
tablets on the ground. Then, he set fire to the
golden calf. He ground the melted gold into
powder. Then he threw it into the water and
forced the people to drink it.

GOD'S GLORY

"Then Moses said, 'Now, please show me your greatness.' The Lord answered, 'I will cause all my goodness to pass in front of you. . . . But you cannot see my face . . . and stay alive.'" EXODUS 33:18-20

The Lord told Moses, "Prepare two stone tablets. Bring them to Me on the mountain. I will write down My rules once more." Moses stayed forty more days on the mountain with God. The Lord God in all His glory passed by Moses.
But Moses did not see God's face.

The Lord said, "I am a kind and loving God. I do not get angry quickly. I forgive My people for their sins. But, I remember to punish the wicked."

Moses bowed to the ground and worshiped God.

"Lord, please forgive these stubborn, sinful people," Moses prayed.

The Lord said, "All right. I will make an agreement with you. I will do miracles that have never been seen before. The people will see My power. And you must obey My rules."

THE HOLY TENT

"Then Moses said to the people of Israel, . . . 'The Lord has given Bezalel the skill, ability and knowledge to do all kinds of work . . . to build the Holy Tent.'" Exodus 35:30, 31; 36:1

When Moses returned to camp, his face glowed like the sun. God had given Moses the plans for building a Holy Tent. Now, the people would have a place to worship God.

Moses said to the people, "Everyone who wants to give may bring a gift to God. This will help us to build the Holy Tent." The people brought jewelry of silver and gold. They brought colorful cloth and special wood. They gave more than what was needed to build the house of God!

Then God filled a man named Bezalel with His Spirit. He gave him and others special skills to build the Holy Tent.

THE TRAVELING CHURCH

"Then the cloud covered the Meeting Tent. The greatness of the Lord filled the Holy Tent. . . . When the cloud rose from the Holy Tent, the Israelites would begin to travel." EXODUS 40:34, 36

When the tent was completed, Moses held a special service. He sprinkled oil on the Holy Box with God's laws in it. Moses anointed everything in the tent with oil to make it holy.

Moses washed Aaron and his sons with water.
Then Moses poured the anointing oil on
them, to prepare them for service to God.
The Lord had chosen them to be His priests.
After seven days, Aaron offered sacrifices for
the sins of the people.

Aaron lifted up his hands and blessed the
people. Then, the Lord's glory came to all the
people.
Holy fire came upon the altar and burned up
the sacrifices. When the people saw this, they
shouted for joy. Then they bowed down to
worship the Lord.

Since the Israelites moved from place to
place, the Holy Tent was like a "traveling
church." It stood in the middle of camp for
everyone to see. God's great cloud covered it
all through the day. At night, the Lord
showed His presence in a blaze of fire above
His tent. Whenever God's great cloud or holy
fire moved, the Israelites followed it.

SPECIAL HELP

*"The Lord said to Moses, 'Bring me 70 of Israel's older leaders. . . .
I will take some of the Spirit that is in you. And I will give it to them.
They will help you care for the people.'"* NUMBERS *11:16, 17*

The Israelites started complaining about all
their troubles in the desert. They forgot to be
thankful for God's daily miracles.
The Lord became angry. His fire burned up
part of the camp. The people cried out to
Moses for help.
When Moses prayed, the fire stopped.

The Lord told Moses to bring seventy of
Israel's leaders to the Holy Tent and He
would give him some help.
The Lord spoke through the great cloud.
Then, the Holy Spirit came upon them all,
and they prophesied. Moses was glad to have
help.

Next, the Lord taught the grumblers a lesson. They had complained about having no meat. So God sent them quail to eat. They had to eat it every day for a month. And they hated it. It made them terribly sick.

EYE SPY

" 'The land we went to explore is very good. . . . Don't be afraid of the people in that land! . . . They have no protection, but we have the Lord.' " NUMBERS 14:7, 9

One day the Israelites camped close to Canaan. This was the land God had promised them.

Moses sent twelve men to scout out the land. "Look at the land. Notice where the cities are. See how strong the enemy is. Then, bring back your report," Moses told them.

The twelve spies scouted the land for forty days.
They returned to camp with samples of fruit.
The people were excited to see the huge
grape clusters and fresh figs.
The men said, "The land is beautiful, with
plenty of fruit and water. But . . . the people
who live there are like giants."

"We felt like grasshoppers beside them," said
ten of the spies. "They are too strong for us."
But two spies, Caleb and Joshua, said, "Don't
be afraid of the people in the land. The Lord
is on our side. He will lead us into the land."
But the Israelites believed what the ten spies
said and started grumbling again.

The Lord said to Moses, "How long will it be
before these people believe Me?"
The Lord was very angry.
He made the Israelites wander in the
wilderness for forty more years. Only Joshua,
Caleb, and the younger generations were
allowed to enter into the Promised Land.

A DONKEY THAT TALKS

"Then the Spirit of God entered him. And Balaam gave this message: . . . 'Anyone who blesses you will be blessed. And anyone who curses you will be cursed.'" NUMBERS 24:2, 3, 9

Now, the surrounding countries feared Israel. King Balak was terrified to see them marching near his land. Balak wanted to drive Israel back into the desert. He sent a message to Balaam, the prophet: "Come and curse these Israelites. I will give you a great reward."

But God warned Balaam. "Do not curse Israel,"
He said. "I have already blessed them."
God told Balaam, "Go to Balak. But only do
what I tell you." Balaam saddled his donkey
and traveled toward Balak's country.

God knew Balaam really wanted the reward
from Balak. God sent an angel with a sword
to stop Balaam. Balaam's donkey saw the
angel but Balaam didn't.
The donkey ran off the road. Balaam hit him
and forced him back onto the road.

The Lord made Balaam's donkey talk. "Why are you hitting me?"
Balaam said, "You're making me look like a fool!"
"Have I ever done this before?" said the donkey.

Suddenly, Balaam saw the angel and
fell to the ground. "I have sinned," said
Balaam. "I did not see you blocking the
road." So Balaam blessed Israel instead of
cursing them.

BE STRONG! BE BRAVE!

"So the Lord said to Moses, 'Take Joshua son of Nun. My Spirit is in him. Put your hand on him. . . . Let him share your honor. Then all the Israelites will obey him.'" NUMBERS *27:18, 20*

After Moses died, Joshua became the Israelites' leader. The Lord told Joshua to cross the Jordan River and lead the people into the Promised Land.

The Lord said, "Joshua, be strong and brave! Don't be afraid. I will be with you everywhere you go."

Joshua told the people, "Get ready. In three days, we will cross the Jordan River."

The people answered, "Anything you tell us to do, we will obey."

They traveled to the Jordan River and camped there before crossing it. Joshua said, "Tomorrow, God will do amazing things."

The Israelites prayed.

They believed God would perform a miracle for them to enter the Promised Land.

The next day, Joshua told the priests to go to the river and step into the water. The priests obeyed Joshua. They carried the Holy Box from the Holy Tent to show that God was with them. At the moment they stepped into the river, the water stopped flowing.

The priests walked to the middle of the river
and waited. All the people of Israel crossed
the Jordan River on dry ground.
Then the priests carried the Holy Box to the
other side. As soon as their feet touched the
riverbank, the water became deep again.

WALLS THAT FALL

"The Lord spoke to Joshua. He said, 'Look, I have given you Jericho. . . . The walls of the city will fall.'" JOSHUA 6:2, 5

Joshua was near the city of Jericho.
Suddenly, a man with a sword appeared.
"I am the Commander of the Lord's army,"
he said. "Take off your sandals. You are
standing on holy ground."
Joshua realized it was the Lord. So Joshua
removed his shoes and bowed down.

The Lord told Joshua how to capture the city
in seven days.

Following God's plan, the priests led the
Israelite army around Jericho. Once a day,
the soldiers silently circled the city.

On the seventh day, they marched around
Jericho seven times. Then the priests blew
their trumpets.
Joshua cried out, "Shout, for the Lord has
given you the city!"
When everyone shouted, the strong walls
shook and fell down. Israel won the battle.

STOLEN TREASURE

" 'The Lord, the God of Israel, says some of you are keeping things he commanded you to destroy. You will never defeat your enemies until you throw away those things.'" JOSHUA 7:13

There was great treasure in Jericho. So Joshua said it must be given to the Lord.
Everything else was to be destroyed.
But a man named Achan disobeyed. He found a beautiful coat and some shiny gold and silver. He took the treasure to his tent and hid it. Achan robbed God!

Later, Joshua sent a small army to attack the tiny town of Ai. But Ai defeated them. And the Israelites were afraid.

Joshua prayed, "Lord, why did You let this happen to us?"

The Lord told Joshua, "Israel has stolen from Me. I will not help you defeat your enemies unless you obey Me."

God showed Joshua that Achan was the
robber.
The treasure was found in Achan's tent.
And he was stoned to death for stealing.
Afterwards, Joshua sent another army
against Ai. This time, Israel won the battle
easily.

TWO WOMEN SAVE ISRAEL

"On that day Deborah and Barak son of Abinoam sang this song: 'The leaders led Israel. The people volunteered to go to battle. Praise the Lord! I myself will sing to the Lord. I will make music to the LORD, the God of Israel.'" JUDGES 5:1-3

After Joshua died, the Israelites forgot their promises to serve the Lord God.
They prayed to gods of wood and stone.
Israel became weak without God's strength.
An evil general, named Sisera, attacked Israel with his mighty army.
Finally the Israelites begged God for help.

At that time, Deborah was a leader in Israel. God's Spirit was upon her, and she was very wise. Deborah told the people what God wanted to say to them.

She told a man named Barak, "Call out the men to fight. The Lord will help you defeat Sisera."

But Barak was afraid.

Deborah said, "Since you don't trust God for the victory, a woman will win this war." When they went to battle, Israel's army surprised the enemy.

Sisera's army ran away.

Sisera ran to a tent that belonged to a woman named Jael.

"Come in, General Sisera," Jael said. "You may hide here."

General Sisera was thirsty and tired from running. Jael gave him a jug of milk, and he slept soundly.

While Sisera was sleeping, Jael killed the evil general. Then she showed Barak what she had done.

The women Deborah and Jael won the victory for Israel because they trusted the Lord.

GOD'S ARMY

"Then Gideon said to the Lord, 'If you are pleased with me, give me proof. Show me that it is really you talking with me.'" JUDGES *6:17*

For seven years, the Midianites attacked Israel. Then the angel of the Lord appeared to Gideon and said, "I have given you the strength to save Israel."

Gideon said, "Lord, why me? I am poor and
unimportant. What can I do?"
The Lord said, "I will be with you."
But, Gideon was unsure.

One night, Gideon asked God for proof.
He said, "I will put some wool outside.
Tomorrow, if the wool is wet and the ground
is dry, I will know that You are with me."

The next morning, the wool was full of water
and the ground was dry.
Gideon still doubted God. He said,
"Tomorrow let the ground be wet and the
wool be dry."
And that is exactly what God did.

The Spirit of God entered Gideon. After that, thousands of men stepped forward to follow him. The Lord said to Gideon, "Your army is too large. Tell the men who are afraid that they may go home."
Finally, Gideon chose 300 men to be in his army. God told him to give each man a trumpet and a jar with a burning torch inside.

That night, Gideon's small army surrounded the enemy camp. All at once, Gideon and his men blew their trumpets and smashed their jars.

They shouted, "A sword for the Lord and for Gideon!"

The scared Midianite army ran away.

SAMSON'S SECRET

"The angel of the Lord appeared to Manoah's wife. He said, 'You have not been able to have children. But you will become pregnant and have a son! . . . You must never cut his hair because he will be a Nazirite. He will be given to God from birth.'" JUDGES 13:3, 5

One day the angel of the Lord surprised Manoah and his wife.
"Soon you will have a son," he said.
"You must never cut his hair. This will be a sign that he belongs to God. Your son will help rescue Israel from her enemies."
Manoah and his wife named their baby Samson.

When Samson grew up, the Spirit of the Lord
gave him great power. He became the
strongest man that ever lived. One afternoon
Samson killed a lion with his bare hands.
Then he used his great strength to fight
against God's enemies. For many years,
Samson was a leader in Israel.

Samson loved a woman named Delilah.
Enemies paid Delilah to find out the secret of
Samson's strength. Delilah tricked Samson,
and he said, "My hair has never been cut."
While he was sleeping, Delilah called a man
to cut Samson's hair. When Samson woke up,
his strength was gone.
The enemy made Samson blind and put him
in prison.

One day Samson's enemies brought him to a big party in honor of their false gods. They wanted to make fun of him. Samson prayed, "Lord, give me strength again!"
Samson pushed on the pillars that held up the ceiling. And the building crashed down on the evil people. The Lord had helped Samson defeat the enemy one last time.

A DAUGHTER'S LOVE

"But Ruth said, 'Don't ask me to leave you! Don't beg me not to follow you! Every place you go, I will go. Every place you live, I will live. Your people will be my people. Your God will be my God.'" RUTH 1:16

Naomi lived in the country of Moab. It was far away from her hometown of Bethlehem. Naomi was sad because her husband and sons had died. She decided to move back to Bethlehem. Naomi told her daughter-in-law Ruth, "I am old and poor. You are young and beautiful. Stay here in your own country and remarry."

Naomi was a good woman, and Ruth loved
her dearly. Ruth said, "I will stay with you. I
will go wherever you go. Your people will be
my people. Your God will be my God." So
Ruth left her friends and family to travel with
Naomi to the city of Bethlehem.
The two widows were very poor.

Ruth gathered grain in a nearby field, so they would have food to eat. A rich man named Boaz owned the land.
He noticed Ruth working hard in his field. Boaz saw that Ruth was kind to her mother-in-law. Boaz married Ruth, and they had a baby boy. Now Naomi and Ruth were happy because God had given them a new family.

HANNAH'S PRAYER

"'I prayed for this child. The Lord answered my prayer and gave him to me. . . . He will belong to the Lord all his life. . . .'" 1 SAMUEL 1:27, 28

Hannah wanted a baby very much.
She prayed to God for a son. She promised he would do God's work all his life.
Eli, the priest, saw Hannah praying. "Go in peace," he said. "May God answer your prayer."
And the Lord God blessed Hannah with a baby boy. She named him Samuel, which means "Asked of God."

Hannah remembered her promise to God.
When Samuel was still a small child, she
took him to Eli at the Holy Tent.
And Samuel lived with the priest.
God was good to Hannah because she kept
her promise. Hannah became the mother of
three sons and two daughters.

SAMUEL HEARS A VOICE

"Samuel said, 'Speak, Lord. I am your servant, and I am listening.'"
1 SAMUEL 3:10

One night, little Samuel was sleeping in the
Holy Tent. A voice called his name.
Samuel ran to Eli and said, "Here I am.
What do you want me to do?"
Eli said, "I didn't call you. Go back to bed."

Samuel went back to bed. Soon, he heard the
voice calling him again. Samuel rushed to
Eli's side. "I am here. You called me," he
said.

"No, I didn't," Eli said. "Go lie down."
Eli realized the Lord was calling Samuel.
Eli said, "When you hear the voice again,
say, 'Speak, Lord. I am listening.'"

So, the Lord spoke to Samuel.
From then on, Samuel gave God's messages
to the people. And all the messages came
true. Samuel was a prophet and ruler in
Israel for many years.

TALL SAUL

"'You must honor the Lord and serve him. You must obey his commands. Both you and the king ruling over you must follow the Lord your God. If you do, it will be well with you.'" 1 SAMUEL *12:14*

When Samuel was old, the people asked him to choose a king to lead them. They said, "All the other countries have kings. We want a king, too."

Samuel was not pleased.

"Do what the people ask," the Lord told him. "But warn them a king will bring trouble."

At this time, there lived a young man named
Saul. Several of his father's donkeys had
wandered away, and Saul was searching for
them. Saul went to see Samuel, the prophet.
He hoped the wise man would help him find
the donkeys. When Samuel saw the tall,
young Saul, the Lord said, "Anoint this man
ruler over My people."

Samuel poured oil over Saul's head and anointed him the first king of Israel. Then the Spirit of the Lord entered Saul, and he prophesied. Saul was a good king, as long as he listened to Samuel and obeyed God.

THE SINGING SHEPHERD

"'God does not see the same way people see. People look at the outside of a person, but the Lord looks at the heart.'" 1 Samuel 16:7

Time passed. Saul became proud and stubborn. He no longer obeyed God, and the Spirit left him. The Lord spoke to Samuel, "Go to the home of Jesse in Bethlehem. I have chosen one of his sons to be king." Samuel felt sorry for Saul. But he obeyed the Lord.

Samuel met seven of Jesse's sons. But God did
not choose any of them.
Samuel did not understand.
God told Samuel, "I don't look at how
handsome or tall a man is. I see a man's
heart and thoughts."

Samuel asked Jesse to send for his youngest
son, David, who was taking care of the sheep.
The Lord told Samuel to anoint David.
Samuel poured the oil on David's head.
The Lord's Spirit entered David. Samuel told
David that someday he would be king.

Meanwhile, King Saul was sad and worried because God's Spirit was not with him. Saul's servant said, "Send for David, the shepherd. He sings and plays the harp. The music will make you feel better." Saul sent for David. And whenever David sang and played, King Saul's sadness left him.

SONGS OF PRAISE

"Let everything that breathes praise the Lord." PSALM 150:6

David loved the Lord with all his heart.
He wrote many songs of praise while caring
for his sheep. He sang: "Lord, Your name is
the most wonderful name in all the earth.
Even children and babies sing praises to
You."

David wrote, "Children, come and listen to
me. I will teach you to worship the Lord."
He sang: "Every good thing I have comes
from the Lord."
David said, "I praise the Lord at all times.
His praise is always on my lips."

BIG MAN, LITTLE MAN

"'The Lord saved me from a lion and a bear. He will also save me from this Philistine. . . . The Lord does not need swords or spears to save people. The battle belongs to him! . . .'" 1 SAMUEL 17: 37, 47

"David!" Jesse called. "Take this bread and cheese to your big brothers. They are with Saul's army fighting against the evil Philistines.
Go, see how your brothers are doing. Then hurry home with your report."
Jesse knew he could trust David to obey him.

One of the Philistines was a giant man
named Goliath. Every day Goliath shouted,
"I dare any man in Israel to fight me! If your
man wins, then we will be your slaves. But if
I win, then you must be our slaves."

No man in Israel would stand up to Goliath.
David asked, "How can we let this man
shame God's army? I will fight Goliath."
Saul said, "You're just a boy."
"The Lord will save me from this giant,"
David answered.
Saul put his battle clothes on David, but the
boy couldn't **move in them.**

David took off Saul's armor.
Then, he picked five stones from a stream
and put them in a pouch.
David went to fight Goliath with his
shepherd's stick and his sling.
Goliath laughed, "Are you going to hit me
with your stick?"

David answered, "You come after me with a
sword and spears. But I stand before you in
the name of the Lord."
David put a stone into his sling and swung it
around. The stone struck Goliath, and the
giant fell to the ground. The Lord helped
David win the victory.

A DANCE OF JOY

"David danced with all his might before the Lord." 2 SAMUEL 6:14

David was a hero. Everyone loved him.
But Saul was very jealous.
Saul wanted to kill David so the people
couldn't make him king.
For many years, David hid from Saul.
And the Lord kept David safe.

When Saul died, David became king of
Israel. And he built a palace in Jerusalem.
The Holy Box of God was then moved to
Jerusalem. As the priests brought the Holy
Box into the city, the Israelites shouted for joy
and played their instruments. And David
danced with all his might before the Lord.

The Holy Box of God was put in a tent.
But King David said to Nathan the prophet,
"I want to build a temple for God."
That night, the Lord told Nathan, "Tell David
that his son will build My temple. And I will
make his kingdom last forever."

Nathan told David what God had said.
David praised God in the Holy Tent when he
heard this message.
"Lord, You have done great miracles for
Israel. And You have promised good things to
me, Your servant. Please, bless my family
forever!"

THE SPIRIT FILLS THE TEMPLE

"The Lord's glory filled the Temple." 2 Chronicles 7:1

Before David died, he told his son Solomon,
"Obey the Lord and you will be successful."
And that's what Solomon did.
Then the Lord came to Solomon in a dream.
God said, "Ask for anything, and I will give it
to you."
Solomon said, "Give me the wisdom to rule
Your people in the right way."

The Lord made King Solomon a wise ruler.
Then, Solomon built a house for God in
Jerusalem. It was called the temple.
The temple was like God's tent in the desert.
But it was much bigger and made of stone.
It sat high on a hilltop, called Mount Zion,
for everyone to see.

When the temple was completed, God's
people had a special service. The Holy Box
was placed in the Most Holy Place.
Everyone sang songs of praise.
The house of God filled with a cloud to show
the glory and presence of God.

King Solomon knelt to pray.
He asked God to bless the temple.
The Lord spoke to Solomon, "I have heard
your prayer. I have made this temple holy.
And I will bless this house as long as My
people obey Me!"

ELIJAH THE PROPHET

"The Lord, the God of Israel, says, 'That jar of flour will never become empty. The jug will always have oil in it. This will continue until the day the Lord sends rain to the land.'" 1 KINGS 17:14

While Solomon was king, Israel was a land of peace and great riches. But after Solomon died, the land was divided into the kingdoms of Israel and Judah.

Evil kings ruled for many years. Ahab was the worst king of all. He and his wicked wife, Jezebel, worshiped the false god Baal.

Ahab and Jezebel believed Baal ruled over
the rain and sunshine.

Now, Elijah was a mighty prophet who
served the true God of Israel. The Lord gave
Elijah a message for Ahab: "There will be no
rain in Israel until the Lord commands it."
Ahab became very angry when he heard
Elijah's words.

The Lord God led Elijah to a brook. God sent
birds with bread and meat for Elijah to eat.
Elijah drank water from the brook.
Many days passed without rain.
The plants died and the land became dry.
When the brook dried up, too, God sent
Elijah to the home of a poor widow.

Elijah asked the woman for a cup of water and a piece of bread.
"All I have is enough flour and oil to make one last meal for my son and me," she said.
"Bake me a small loaf of bread first," said Elijah. "Then, cook for yourself."

"Don't worry," Elijah said. "Trust God to take care of you." The woman shared her little bit of bread with Elijah, and the Lord blessed her with more. The jar of flour and the jug of oil were never empty. So Elijah, the widow, and her son had enough food for each day.

VICTORY ON MOUNT CARMEL

"Elijah stood before the people. He said, 'How long will you try to serve both Baal and the Lord? If the Lord is the true God, follow him. But if Baal is the true God, follow him!'" 1 KINGS 18:21

There was no rain in Israel for three years. The people had no food. One day Elijah told Ahab that God would send rain soon. Ahab called Elijah "Israel's troublemaker." But Elijah said, "You're the cause of Israel's hunger. You disobeyed God by telling His people to bow before Baal."

Elijah told Ahab to meet him on Mount
Carmel. Elijah also invited all Israel and the
prophets of Baal. Elijah told the people, "You
can't serve both God and Baal."

He told the prophets of Baal, "Build two
altars. You offer a sacrifice to Baal, and I will
offer a sacrifice to the Lord."

Then Elijah said, "You pray to your god and I will pray to the Lord. The god who answers with fire is the true God."

The prophets of Baal built an altar. But when they prayed, nothing happened. Baal did not speak because he was only a statue.

Elijah built an altar. He poured water on the
stones, the wood, and the sacrifice.
Elijah prayed, "Lord, I ask You to show these
people that You are God."
Fire came down from heaven. It burned up
the sacrifice, the wood, the stones, and the
water. When the people saw this, they cried
"The Lord, He is God!"
Elijah prayed again, and the Lord sent rain.

A WIND AND A WHISPER

"Then a very strong wind blew. . . . But the Lord was not in the wind. . . . After the fire, there was a quiet, gentle voice." 1 KINGS 19:11, 12

Queen Jezebel was angry because God had answered Elijah's prayer.
She sent Elijah a message: "Tomorrow you will die." Elijah ran away to save his life. He walked through a desert for one whole day. He was tired and hungry. At last he lay down and fell asleep.

The Lord was kind to Elijah. Twice, He sent
an angel to cheer him up.
The angel touched him and said, "Get up
and eat, Elijah. If you don't, the trip will be
too hard for you."
Elijah opened his eyes and saw a loaf of
bread and a jug of water. The food made him
strong enough to walk for forty more days.

Finally, Elijah came to Mount Sinai, the
mountain of God. The Lord said, "Stand in
front of Me. I will pass by you."
A great wind swept by Elijah, but the Lord
was not in it. Elijah saw an earthquake, but
the Lord was not in it. A fire passed by, too,
but the Lord was not in it, either.

After the fire, Elijah heard a soft voice. He
knew it was the voice of the Lord.
"Why are you running, Elijah?" the Lord
asked him.
"I feel afraid and alone," Elijah said.
The Lord said, "Go pour oil on Elisha. He will
be your helper."

THE BATTLE IS THE LORD'S

"The Lord says this to you: 'Don't be afraid or discouraged. . . . The battle is not your battle. It is God's battle. . . .'" 2 CHRONICLES 20:15

During the days of Elijah, there lived a good king named Jehoshaphat.

The Lord was with Jehoshaphat because he obeyed God's commands. Jehoshaphat removed the false gods in Judah. Then he sent out priests to teach the people how to serve the Lord.

One day, a large army wanted to fight God's people. Jehoshaphat called the people to a special time of prayer.

He told the people not to eat any food that day. People traveled from every town in Judah to pray with Jehoshaphat in Jerusalem.

Jehoshaphat prayed, "Lord, we have no
power against this army. Please, help us."
Then the Spirit entered the man Jahaziel.
Jahaziel said, "Don't be afraid for the Lord is
with you. You will not have to fight. The
battle is the Lord's."
The people worshiped the Lord.

The next morning, Jehoshaphat said to his army, "Believe in the Lord and you will stand strong." As the army of Judah marched toward the enemy, they sang and praised God. Then God caused the enemy soldiers to fight each other. So God's people won the battle without fighting.

King Jehoshaphat and his people gathered
everything the enemy left behind. They
carried away money, jewelry, and clothes.
The people praised the Lord for His help and
blessing. They were happy because their
enemies were defeated.

THE CHARIOT OF FIRE

"A group of the prophets at Jericho were watching. They said, 'Elisha now has the spirit Elijah had.'" 2 KINGS 2:15

The work of Elijah was finished. He would soon be taken to heaven.
His helper Elisha walked with him to the Jordan River. Elijah took off his coat. He rolled it up and hit the water.
The water divided to the right and left. They crossed over on dry ground.

179

Elijah said to Elisha, "What can I do for you before I go to heaven?"
Elisha wanted to inherit Elijah's power from God. Elisha said, "Please leave me a double share of your spirit."
"You have asked for a special gift," Elijah said.

Then Elijah said, "If you see me leave, the power from the Spirit will be given to you." Suddenly a chariot and horses of fire appeared. Elisha watched as the chariot took Elijah to heaven in a whirlwind. Elisha did not see his friend anymore. But Elijah had dropped his coat. So Elisha picked it up.

Elisha walked to the Jordan River.
He hit the water with Elijah's coat.
The water parted just as it had for Elijah.
Elisha now had the same power that Elijah
had used. The Lord had chosen Elisha to
replace the great prophet Elijah.

A DEAD BOY SNEEZES

"When Elisha entered the room, he shut the door. Only he and the child were in the room. Then Elisha prayed to the Lord. . . . The child sneezed seven times and opened his eyes." 2 KINGS 4:33, 35

Elisha traveled throughout Israel. He taught the people to worship the Lord.
In one city, a wealthy woman invited Elisha to her home for dinner. Whenever Elisha passed through that city, he visited the woman and her husband.

Later, the woman and her husband built a
small room on the roof for Elisha. They put a
bed, a chair, a table, and a lampstand in it.
Now Elisha had a place to rest.

One day, Elisha said to the woman, "What can
I do for you? You have been so kind to me."
The woman said, "There is nothing I need."
Elisha said to her, "God will give you a son
next year."
And Elisha's words came true.

Several years later, the woman's child cried,
"My head hurts!"
The sick boy died in his mother's arms.
The woman sadly carried him into Elisha's
room. Then, she quickly saddled the donkey
and hurried to find Elisha.

When the boy's mother reached Elisha, she cried for her son. She said, "Elisha, I won't leave unless you come with me!"
So, Elisha followed her home. Elisha prayed over the boy. The child sneezed seven times and opened his eyes. The woman praised the Lord for bringing her son back to life.

A LITTLE GIRL HELPS

"Naaman . . . stood before Elisha and said, 'Look. I now know there is no God in all the earth except in Israel!'" 2 KINGS 5:15

Naaman was a hero and leader of a foreign army. But an ugly disease covered his skin. Naaman and his wife had an Israelite servant. One day, the little servant girl said, "I wish my master would meet the prophet Elisha. He could heal Naaman."

Naaman listened to the little girl.
He traveled many miles to Elisha's home in
Israel. He waited at Elisha's door. But the
prophet didn't come.
Instead, Elisha sent a messenger to speak
with Naaman.

The messenger said, "Wash in the Jordan River seven times and you will be healed." Naaman was a proud man. He was upset that Elisha did not talk to him. One of Naaman's servants said gently, "Sir, the prophet didn't ask you to do something difficult. He said to wash, and you will be well."

So Naaman dipped seven times in the Jordan River. His skin became healthy. He hurried back to Elisha's house.

"Look! Your God healed me," Naaman told Elisha. "I will serve no other God, but the Lord."

THE BIG FISH NEAR TARSHISH

"'Lord, I will praise and thank you while I give sacrifices to you. I will make promises to you. And I will do what I promise. Salvation comes from the Lord!'" JONAH 2:9

After Elisha died, God spoke to another prophet. His name was Jonah.
"Go to Ninevah, the great city in Assyria," God said. "Preach to the people."

Jonah did not want to preach to his enemies.
So he ran away from the Lord.
He boarded a ship to Tarshish. Then Jonah
fell asleep, thinking he was safe.
But the Lord sent a great storm while the ship
was at sea. The ship was about to sink.
The terrified sailors prayed to their gods.

The captain woke Jonah, "Get up! Pray to
your God! Maybe He will save us!"
Jonah said, "It's my fault this storm has
come. I ran away from God. Throw me into
the water and the storm will stop."
So they threw Jonah into the sea.
And the water became calm.

The men on the ship greatly feared Jonah's
God. They promised to serve the Lord.
Meanwhile, Jonah cried for God to save him.
And the Lord caused a big fish to swallow
him up.
Jonah lived inside the fish for three days.
There he praised the Lord for saving his life.

Jonah promised to obey God.
Then the Lord caused the fish to spit him out
onto dry land.
Jonah took God's word to the people of
Ninevah.
The people turned away from their sins and
believed in the Lord.

THE KING OF JUDAH

"'Don't be afraid of what you have heard. Don't be frightened. . . .'"
2 Kings 19: 6

Many years passed. Hezekiah became the king of Judah. He obeyed the Lord. Hezekiah helped the people remember their promises to God, and the Lord blessed them.

One time the Assyrian army marched toward
Jerusalem. So God's people built stronger
walls around the city.
Hezekiah told the people, "Don't be afraid.
God is with us."

God's people watched from the walls as the enemy army surrounded their city.
The enemy captain yelled, "Don't listen to Hezekiah. Your God can't save you!"
Hezekiah told his people, "Don't answer him." The people kept quiet.
Then Hezekiah went to the temple to pray.

Hezekiah called for Isaiah the prophet.
Isaiah said, "Don't be scared. The Lord will
defend and save you."
That night, God sent an angel to attack and
kill the enemy. So the Lord saved Hezekiah
and the people of Judah.

HEZEKIAH'S HEALING

". . . The Lord, the God of your ancestor David, says: 'I have heard your prayer. And I have seen your tears. So I will heal you. . . . '"
2 KINGS 20:5

Hezekiah became sick with a deadly disease. Isaiah said, "Get ready to die. The Lord says you won't get better."
Hezekiah cried to the Lord, "God, please remember how I've always tried to obey You." He begged God to give him a longer life.

God gave Isaiah a message for Hezekiah.
Isaiah said, "You will be healed. The Lord
will add many years to your life."
Isaiah told Hezekiah to put medicine on his
body. Then Isaiah prayed for Hezekiah, and
he was healed.

THE BOY KING

" 'You became sorry in the Lord's presence for what you had done . . .
This is why I have heard you, says the Lord.' " 2 KINGS 22:19

Before long, the people of Judah turned from
God to fortune-tellers and witchcraft.
At this time, Josiah became king.
He was only eight years old!
But he loved the Lord and tried to live right.

When Josiah was old enough to rule, he
hired workers to fix up God's house.
One day, the workers found an old scroll that
had been lost for many years.
A priest took it to Josiah. "Here's a book of
God's rules!" the priest said. Then a servant
read God's Word to Josiah.

Josiah was very upset.
His people were not following God's rules!
"Ask God what we should do," Josiah told the
priest. The priest went to Huldah, a prophetess.
Huldah gave him God's message. "The people
have sinned. But the Lord will not harm
Josiah because he is sorry for their sins."

Josiah called all the people to the temple.
He read the book of God's rules for everyone
to hear. Then the people promised to obey
God's Word. And they destroyed all their
false gods.
There was never another king like Josiah.
He obeyed the Lord with all his heart.

A PROPHET WHO CRIED

"The Lord says . . . 'You will . . . pray to me. And I will listen to you. . . . When you search for me with all your heart, you will find me!'" JEREMIAH *29: 10-13*

Jeremiah was a prophet of God.
The Lord gave him a sad message to give to the people of Jerusalem.
"Soon the king of Babylon will capture you."
But the people didn't listen.

One day King Nebuchadnezzar came from
Babylon with his mighty army.
He attacked Jerusalem.
He took the temple treasures and many of
the people to Babylon.
Jeremiah cried when God's words came true.

Jeremiah wrote a letter to comfort the
prisoners in Babylon.
He told them, "The Lord says: 'I will change
your sadness into joy. I will bring you back to
Jerusalem when you learn to follow Me with
all your heart.'"

THE FIRE PIT

"Then Nebuchadnezzar said . . . 'These three men . . . were willing to die rather than serve or worship any god other than their own. . . . No other god can save his people like this.'" DANIEL *3:28, 29*

In Babylon, King Nebuchadnezzar asked for four young men from Judah to serve in his palace. Daniel and his three friends were chosen. They studied hard to learn the king's language. And God helped them.

King Nebuchadnezzar had a huge gold statue
made. He ordered everyone in Babylon to
bow down and worship the statue.
"Anyone who doesn't will be thrown into a
fire pit," the king said.
Daniel's three friends would not bow and
worship the golden statue.

When the king found out, he was very angry.
He called for Shadrach, Meshach, and
Abednego.
"Why won't you worship my statue?" the
king asked.
They answered, "We worship only God."
So the king had them thrown into a fire pit.

When the king looked into the pit, he saw
four men instead of three. They were walking
around in the fire and were not burned.
"The fourth man looks like a son of the gods,"
the king said. "Praise the God of Shadrach,
Meshach, and Abednego.
He has saved them from the fire."

A SECRET MESSAGE

"The Most High God rules over the kingdoms of men. And the Most High God sets anyone he wants over those kingdoms." DANIEL 5:21

Many years later, the king's son had a big party to honor the false gods.
He used golden cups that were stolen from the Lord's temple.
Suddenly the hand of God wrote a message on the wall. Everyone was afraid.

The wise men in the kingdom could not
understand the writing.
So the king's son sent for Daniel because he
knew how to explain dreams.
"If you can read this writing, I will give you a
great reward," the king told Daniel.
"Please, keep your gifts," Daniel said.

"You have offended the Most High God,"
Daniel told the king's son. "You have used His
holy things in a wrong way. God has sent this
message to tell you your kingdom will be
taken away from you."
And God's words came true.

DANIEL IN THE LIONS' PIT

"Then King Darius wrote . . . . 'All of you must fear and respect the God of Daniel. . . . God saved Daniel from the power of the lion.'"
DANIEL 6:25–27

The next ruler was King Darius. He knew
Daniel was wise and truthful. He chose
Daniel to help him rule the kingdom.
The other leaders were jealous.
They thought of a way to trap Daniel.

These men knew Daniel prayed to the Lord
each day. So they tricked the king into
signing a law about prayer.
It said no one should pray to any god but
King Darius!
Anyone who disobeyed the law would be
thrown into the lions' pit.

Daniel heard about the law, but it did not
stop him from praying to God.
The men told the king about Daniel.
The king was very sad and upset.
He didn't want to punish his loyal helper.
But he couldn't change the foolish law.
Daniel was thrown into the lions' pit.

The next morning Darius hurried to the
lions' pit. He called, "Daniel, has the God
you worship been able to save you?"
"Yes," Daniel answered. "God sent an angel
to close the lions' mouths."
Then Darius said, "I'm making a new law.
People in my kingdom must fear your God."

A BEAUTY QUEEN

"'You may have been chosen queen for just such a time as this.'"
ESTHER 4:14

The king of Persia needed a queen.
All the prettiest girls in the kingdom were
brought before him.
Esther was the most beautiful girl of all.
She was chosen to be the queen.

No one in the palace knew Esther was Jewish.
"Keep it secret," said Esther's Uncle Mordecai.
Esther always listened to his wise advice.
One day Haman, the king's officer, came to
the city. Everyone bowed down.
But Mordecai would not bow.
He worshiped only the Lord God.

Haman hated Mordecai the Jew.
He made an evil plan to get rid of him.
He tricked the king into signing a law to kill
all the Jewish people living in the land.
Mordecai asked Esther to talk to the king.
Esther said, "There is a law that forbids me
from going to the king without being invited.
I could be punished."

Mordecai said, "God may have let you be
chosen queen for just such a time as this.
Help your people."
Esther prayed for courage. Then she boldly
went to see the king. The king loved Esther
and listened to her.
He punished Haman instead of Mordecai or
Esther. So God used Esther to save her people.

DOUBLE TROUBLE

"'The Lord gave these things to me. And he has taken them away. Praise the name of the Lord.'" JOB 1: 21

Job was a good man. He tried to live right. He prayed every day, "Lord, help me obey You. Please forgive my sins."
God was pleased with Job and blessed him. Job was one of the richest men in the world. Job had eleven grown children. He owned a large farm with many animals and servants.

Satan hated Job for serving the Lord.
One day, Satan stole everything from Job.
Wild men robbed his farm.
The animals were stolen.
His servants were killed.
A tornado took the lives of all his children.
Job lost all he had.

Even though he was sad, Job praised God.
Then Satan caused Job to become sick.
Job's wife said bitterly, "You should blame
God for all this trouble!"
Job said, "Should we take only good things
from God? I don't understand my troubles,
but I won't blame God. I will keep on trusting
Him."

Job said to God, "I know You can do all things."

After that God healed Job's body. And once again God blessed Job with many animals, servants, sons, and daughters.

Job was richer and happier now than he had been before all his troubles.

REBUILDING THE CITY

"The joy of the Lord will make you strong." NEHEMIAH *8:10*

After many years the king of Persia told
God's people, "You may go back to your
homeland and rebuild God's temple!"
The king returned all the valuable treasures
that had been stolen from God's house.
As the people traveled to Jerusalem, they
praised God for keeping His promises.

When they arrived in Jerusalem, God's
people found their city in ruins.
The walls had fallen. The temple was wrecked.
The people were eager to rebuild God's
House. They rebuilt the altar and laid the
temple base. But soon they grew tired and
stopped working.

The Lord spoke to His people through two
men named Haggai and Zechariah.
Haggai told the people, "You have forgotten
God's House. Be brave and work for the
Lord."
Then Zechariah said, "Remember, you won't
do well using your own strength. The power
comes from the Holy Spirit."

The people finished the temple.
But they left the city walls undone.
God caused a man named Nehemiah to
want to rebuild the walls of Jerusalem.
Nehemiah spoke to all the people,
"We are helpless against enemy attacks
without strong walls around our city.
Let's work together to rebuild them."

So each family rebuilt the part of the wall
closest to their home. People outside the city
tried to stop the work on the walls.
They tried to scare the workers.
Nehemiah prayed for God's help.
He chose watchmen to walk around the walls
and guard against enemies.

After fifty-two days of hard work, Jerusalem was a strong, walled city. Then God's people celebrated for seven days. Each day, Ezra, the teacher, read God's Word to them. And they confessed their sins and prayed with loud voices: "You are the only Lord."

The people gave God a tenth of everything they had earned. Then everyone marched around the city on top of the walls, singing and praising God with great joy.
They finally understood what they had been taught.

New Testament

"**G**od will give a son to us. . . . His name will be
Wonderful Counselor, Powerful God, Father Who
Lives Forever, Prince of Peace. . . . He will rule as
king on David's throne. "

—ISAIAH 9:6,7

AN ANGEL VISITS MARY

"God has done what he promised." LUKE 1:55

Mary was a young Jewish girl engaged to Joseph, the carpenter.
Joseph was a good man who loved the Lord.
He would make a fine husband for Mary.
Soon, all their friends and family would celebrate the wedding in Nazareth.
But Mary's life was about to change forever.

One day, God sent an angel to Mary. The
angel said, "Don't be afraid. God is pleased
with you. He has chosen you to be the
mother of Jesus. This Holy Child will be the
King that God promised. And He will be
called the Son of God."

Mary did not understand.
The angel said, "The Holy Spirit will make this happen."
Then he said, "Everyone thought your cousin Elizabeth could not have children.
But she will have a baby in her old age.
God will do everything He promised!"

Mary hurried to Elizabeth and Zechariah's home.
When Elizabeth heard Mary's voice, her unborn baby jumped for joy. And Elizabeth was filled with the Holy Spirit.
She said, "Mary, you are blessed because you believed what God said."

Mary was filled with joy and sang a song:
"My soul praises the Lord; my heart is happy
because God is my Savior."
Mary stayed with Elizabeth and Zechariah
for three months.

ZECHARIAH'S PROPHECY

" 'Now you, child, will be called a prophet of the Most High God. . . .
You will make his people know that they will be saved . . . by having
their sins forgiven.' " LUKE 1:76–77

Several months before Mary's visit, an angel
spoke to Zechariah, the priest.
"Your wife, Elizabeth, will give birth to a son.
And you will name him John."
Zechariah was surprised!

The angel said, "John will help people get ready for the coming of the Lord."
Zechariah doubted. He said, "My wife and I are very old. Are you sure?"
The angel answered, "Because you didn't believe, you will lose your speech until Elizabeth has the baby."

When the baby was born, everyone expected
him to be named Zechariah, after his father.
But Elizabeth said, "No! He will be named
John."
Their friends said, "No one in your family
has that name!"
They asked Zechariah what to call his son.

Zechariah could not speak, so he wrote, "His name is John." Everyone was shocked! Suddenly Zechariah started talking and praising God. He was filled with the Holy Spirit and said, "This child will be a prophet of God. He will point the people to the Savior."

GOD BECAME A BABY BOY

"All the angels were praising God, saying: 'Give glory to God in heaven, and on earth let there be peace to the people who please God.'" Luke 2:13–14

One night, an angel came to Joseph in a dream. "Don't be afraid to take Mary as your wife. The baby inside her is from the Holy Spirit," the angel said. "You will call Him Jesus, which means, *The Lord Saves*."
So Joseph and Mary were married.

The emperor said that all the people must go to their birthplaces to list their names and to pay taxes.

Joseph and Mary traveled many miles to Bethlehem, their hometown. Mary was very tired, but there was no place to rest.

Bethlehem was crowded with people.
And Mary and Joseph had to spend the
night in a stable.
During the night, Mary's baby was born.
Mary loved her wonderful Son.
She wrapped Him in warm clothes and made
a cozy bed for Him in a feedbox.

Some shepherds were watching their sheep in a nearby field. Suddenly an angel appeared. The shepherds were frightened.

The angel said, "Don't be afraid. I am bringing you good news. Tonight your Savior was born in Bethlehem. He is CHRIST the Lord."

Then a choir of angels sang, "Glory to God in heaven."
When the angels left, the shepherds hurried to Bethlehem. They found the baby with Mary and Joseph.
The shepherds were amazed!
They returned to the fields, praising God.

SIMEON PRAISES GOD

"The Holy Spirit told Simeon that he would not die before he saw the Christ." Luke 2:26

Mary and Joseph took Jesus to the temple. An old man named Simeon was there. He was looking for the coming Savior. Simeon praised God when he saw Jesus with Mary and Joseph.

Simeon took Jesus in his arms and said,
"Lord, now I can die in peace. I have seen
the Savior."
An old prophetess named Anna heard
Simeon.
When Anna saw Jesus, she told everyone
that God's promised King had come.

WISE MEN WORSHIP

"When the wise men saw the star, they were filled with joy. They went to the house where the child was. . . . They bowed down and worshiped the child." MATTHEW *2:10, 11*

Mary and Joseph returned to Bethlehem.
Special visitors came from a faraway land to worship Jesus.
They had seen a strange star shining in the sky.

These wise men believed the star meant a
king was born. So they followed the star to
the place where the child was.
The wise men were filled with joy.
They bowed down and worshiped Jesus.
They gave Him precious, costly gifts.

LOST AND FOUND

"The little child began to grow up. He became stronger and wiser, and God's blessings were with him." LUKE 2:40

When Jesus was twelve, He went with Joseph and Mary to Jerusalem. They went for the Passover Feast. After the celebration, many people traveled home together. But Jesus stayed behind in the city. Joseph and Mary did not know it.

Joseph and Mary traveled a whole day before
they realized Jesus was missing.
They went back to Jerusalem to look for Him.
After three days they found Jesus.
He was in the temple, talking to the teachers.

All who heard Jesus were amazed at His understanding. But Mary and Joseph were upset. His mother said to Him, "Son, we've been looking for You! Why did You worry us?" Jesus said, "Why did you have to look for Me? You should have known I'd be in my Father's House."

Jesus went home with Mary and Joseph. He obeyed them and pleased God.

BAPTIZED!

"'I baptize you with water to show that your hearts and lives have changed. But there is one coming later who is greater than I am. . . . He will baptize you with the Holy Spirit and with fire.'" MATTHEW 3:11

John was the son of Zechariah and Elizabeth. He was no ordinary man. John lived alone in the desert so he could hear the voice of God. He ate wild honey and locusts.
God gave John a message for the people.

Crowds came to hear John preach.
He said, "Turn away from your sins.
Get ready to meet the Son of God."
John told the people to stop stealing and
lying. He said, "Share with people who are
poor and hungry."

John baptized people in the Jordan River.
Many people thought John might be God's
promised King.
John said, "I am not the Savior. I baptize
you with water. But He will baptize you with
the Holy Spirit."

THE DOVE FROM ABOVE

"John said, 'I saw the Spirit come down from heaven. The Spirit looked like a dove and rested on him . . . So I tell people: 'He is the Son of God.'" JOHN 1: 33, 34

Jesus came to John to be baptized. John said, "Look! Here comes the One I've been talking about. He will take away the sins of the world." John was not sure he should be the one to baptize Jesus. But Jesus said, "This is God's plan."

John agreed to baptize Jesus.
When Jesus came up out of the water, the
Holy Spirit came down in the form of a dove
and rested on Him.
Then God's voice spoke from heaven, "You
are My Son and I love You."

DOWN WITH THE DEVIL!

"Jesus said to the devil, 'Go away from me, Satan!' . . . So the devil left Jesus. And then some angels came to Jesus and helped him." MATTHEW 4:10, 11

The Spirit led Jesus into the desert to pray. For forty days Jesus did not eat. When Jesus was tired and hungry, the Devil tried to get Him to disobey God.

The Devil said, "If You are God's Son, change these stones into bread, and eat."

265

Jesus said, "The Scripture says, 'There are things in life more important than food.'"
The Devil told Jesus, "I will give You everything in the world if You worship me."
Jesus answered, "God's Word says, 'You must worship and serve Him only.'"

Satan said, "Prove that You are God's Son.
Jump off the temple roof. God's Word says
His angels will catch You."
Jesus said, "The Scripture also says, 'Don't
test God's power foolishly.'"
Jesus did not disobey God. So, Satan left Him.
Then God sent His angels to feed Jesus.

THE FIRST MIRACLE

"His mother said to the servants, 'Do whatever he tells you to do.'"
JOHN 2:5

Jesus went to a wedding with His mother,
Mary, and some friends. There wasn't enough
wine for the feast. And the bridegroom was
upset.
Mary asked Jesus to help.
Jesus said, "Why come to Me?"

But His mother trusted Jesus to do the right thing. She told the servants, "Do whatever Jesus tells you to do."
Jesus told the servants to fill six big jars with water. When the bridegroom tasted the water, he was surprised. The water had become wine. This was Jesus' first miracle.

FOLLOWING JESUS

"At that time Jesus went off to a mountain to pray. He stayed there all night, praying to God. The next morning, Jesus called his followers to him. He chose 12 of them." LUKE 6:12–13

Jesus went to the synagogue.
He read God's Word to the people.
He said, "The Spirit of the Lord is in Me. God has chosen Me to tell the Good News. He has sent Me to help the sinners and to heal those who are hurting." Then Jesus began to explain God's Word to the people.

One day a crowd of people followed Jesus to
Lake Galilee.
Jesus saw two boats near the shore. The
boats belonged to a group of fishermen—
Peter, Andrew, James, and John.
The men were washing their fishing nets.

Jesus got into Peter's boat and taught the people on the shore. Later, Jesus told Peter, "Put your nets in the deep water, and you will catch fish."

Peter said, "Master, we tried all night, and we didn't catch any fish." But Peter and the other fishermen obeyed Jesus anyway.

They caught so many fish that their nets
broke. The fishermen were amazed.
Peter bowed before Jesus and said, "Lord,
why bother with me? I am a sinner."
Jesus answered, "From now on you will fish
for men."
The men left their boats and followed Jesus.

Jesus chose twelve men to be His closest
friends: Peter and his brother Andrew;
James and his brother John; Philip and
Nathaniel; Matthew, the tax-collector;
Thomas; James, the son of Alphaeus;
Simon; Thaddaeus; and Judas. These
men followed Jesus everywhere.

HEALING THE SICK

"Jesus saw that these men believed. So he said to the sick man, 'Friend, your sins are forgiven.'" Luke 5:20

Jesus was teaching and healing people in a crowded house. Several Jewish leaders were there. They were jealous because Jesus had so many followers.

A paralyzed man could not move from
his bed.
Four good friends carried him to the house
where Jesus was preaching. But the house
was so full of people there was no place to
lay the man.

The friends lowered the man through a hole
in the roof.
Jesus told the paralyzed man, "Your sins are
forgiven."
The Jewish leaders became angry.
"Only God can forgive sins. Who does Jesus
think He is?"

Jesus proved He had the power to forgive
sins. He told the paralyzed man, "Get up.
Take your mat and go home."
The healed man stood up and walked out of
the room.
The people were amazed and praised God.

PREACHING AND TEACHING

"'The thing you should want most is God's kingdom and doing what God wants. Then all these other things you need will be given to you.'"
MATTHEW 6:33

One day Jesus sat on a hillside and taught His followers.
"See the birds in the sky? Your heavenly Father feeds them. God helps the lovely flowers to grow, too."

"If God cares about the birds and flowers, you can trust Him to take care of you," He said. "Remember, the most important thing is to love God and to do what He wants. You please Him by showing love and kindness to others."

"Everyone who obeys Me is like the wise man who built his house on rock," Jesus said. "The rain poured, the water rose, and the wind beat against the house. But the house did not fall because it was built on rock."

"The person who does not obey Me is like a foolish man who built his house on sand," Jesus said.

"When the storm came, the water rose, and the wind hit the house. The house fell with a big crash."

BORN AGAIN

"'For God loved the world so much that he gave his only Son. God gave his Son so that whoever believes in him may not be lost, but have eternal life.'" JOHN 3:16

Nicodemus was an important Jewish leader.
He wanted to talk to Jesus, but he didn't want
any of his friends to see him.
So he came to Jesus in secret at night.
Jesus knew Nicodemus didn't understand
God's plan.

Jesus told Nicodemus, "You must be born
again if you want to go to heaven."
"How can a man be born twice?" Nicodemus
asked.
Jesus explained, "The Holy Spirit will give
you a new life. Everyone who believes in Me
as Savior will go to heaven."

JESUS PUTS AWAY THE DEMONS

"The man that Jesus had healed begged to go with him. But Jesus sent him away, saying, 'Go back home and tell people what God did for you.'" Luke 8:38–39

A man with many demons came to Jesus. This man lived in a cave and wore no clothes. When he saw Jesus, he fell to his knees.

Jesus commanded the evil spirit to come out of the man. When Jesus did this, the demons came out of the man and went into some pigs that were eating nearby.
All the pigs ran into a lake and drowned.

The men who took care of the pigs ran to
town and told everyone what had happened.
The people in town came to see if the crazy
man was cured. He was!
He was listening to Jesus teach.

A TOUCH OF FAITH

"Jesus said . . . 'You are made well because you believed. Go in peace. You will have no more suffering.'" Mark 5:34

A man named Jairus bowed before Jesus and begged, "Please heal my little girl. She's dying!" Jesus went with Jairus, and many people followed.

In the crowd was a woman with a blood
disease. No one could cure her.
The woman had heard about Jesus' miracles.
She believed Jesus could heal her if she could
just reach Him through the crowd.

The woman came up behind Jesus as He
walked with Jairus. She touched the edge of
Jesus' coat.
Instantly, she was healed.
"Who touched Me?" asked Jesus.
Peter said, "Master, anyone in this crowd
could have touched You."

The frightened woman stepped forward.
Jesus said, "You are healed because you
believed."
At the same time, a messenger hurried to
Jairus. "Your daughter is dead!" he cried.
Jesus told Jairus, "Don't be afraid; only believe."

At Jairus's house, everyone was crying.
Jesus said, "Don't cry. The girl is sleeping."
The people laughed at Jesus.
Jesus told the unbelievers to leave the room.
Jesus held the girl's hand and said, "My
child, stand up!" Jairus's daughter stood up.
She was well!

WEEDS AND SEEDS

"Jesus said, 'You have been chosen to know the secret truths of the kingdom of God.'" LUKE 8:10

Jesus told many stories about God's kingdom. "A farmer went out to plant seed," Jesus said. "As he scattered the seed, some fell beside the road. The birds came and ate it all."

"Some seeds fell on rocky ground," He said.
"The hot sun burned those little plants
because they had short roots. Other seeds fell
among weeds that would later choke the
growing plants. But, the seeds that fell on
good soil grew into strong, healthy plants."

The people asked, "What does this story mean?"

Jesus explained, "The seed is the word of God. Some people hear His word; then Satan steals it from them. Other people listen but give up easily when problems come."

"Others let worries and love of money crowd God from their hearts," Jesus said.
"The people who understand God's message are like the seeds planted on good soil. They grow into beautiful 'plants.' Then they tell others the Good News."

TWELVE APOSTLES SENT OUT

"'When you go, preach this: 'The kingdom of heaven is coming soon.' Heal the sick. Give dead people life again. Heal those who have harmful skin diseases. Force demons to leave people.'" MATTHEW 10:7–8

Jesus' twelve closest followers were called apostles.

He gave them power to heal all sicknesses and to drive out demons.

"I give you this gift freely," Jesus said. "So help other people freely."

Jesus said, "Go and tell the people about God's kingdom.
Give dead people life again. Heal the sick.
Don't worry about what to say. The Spirit of God will give you the right words."

The apostles told people to turn away from
their sins and live right.
The twelve men poured olive oil on sick people,
and God healed them. Jesus was pleased.

A BUNCH FOR LUNCH

"All the people ate and were satisfied. And there was much food left."
LUKE 9:17

One day Jesus and His friends sailed across
Lake Galilee. Then they went up on a hill
and sat down.
Many people followed Jesus.
He felt sorry for them because they were like
sheep without a shepherd.

Jesus taught the people all day long.
He said, "Heaven is like a beautiful pearl.
It's worth more than anything else."
After a while, Jesus told His apostles to feed
the people.
Philip answered, "It would take a lot of
money to buy food for this crowd!"

One little boy had five loaves of bread and
two little fish.
He gave them to Andrew.
Andrew told Jesus, "This boy will share his
meal, but it's not enough."
Jesus said, "Tell all the people to sit down for
dinner."

Jesus took the bread and fish.
He looked up to heaven and thanked God.
Then Jesus divided the food and gave it to His
followers. And they shared it with the hungry
people. Everyone had plenty of food to eat.
There were twelve baskets of food left over.

WALKING ON WATER

"Jesus quickly spoke to them. He said, 'Have courage! It is I! Don't be afraid.'" MATTHEW *14:27*

After Jesus fed the large crowd, He sent His apostles by boat to the other side of the lake. Jesus stayed behind until everyone went home. Then He went into the hills to pray.

During the night, a storm came up.
The men in the boat worried that they might
sink. Suddenly a man appeared. He was
walking toward them on the water!
"It's a ghost!" the men cried.
"It is I!" said Jesus. "Do not be afraid."

Peter said, "Lord, can I walk on water, too?"
Jesus said, "Come!"
Peter slowly stepped toward Jesus.
Peter felt the blowing wind and saw the high waves around him.
He became frightened and started to sink.

"Lord, save me!" Peter cried.
Jesus quickly rescued Peter.
"Why did you doubt?" Jesus asked Peter.
When Jesus and Peter got into the boat, the
wind became calm.
"You truly are the Son of God!" said the men.

SEE HIS GLORY

"Then a cloud came and covered them. A voice came from the cloud. The voice said, 'This is my Son, and I love him. Obey him!'" Mark 9:7

Jesus took Peter, James, and John up on a
mountain to pray. While Jesus was praying,
a great change came over Him.
His face began to shine like the sun,
and His clothes became whiter than snow.
His friends saw the glory of Jesus.

Suddenly Moses and Elijah appeared with
Jesus. Jesus' followers were frightened, and a
cloud covered them.
A voice from the cloud said, "This is My Son.
He is the One I have chosen. Obey Him."

A BLIND MAN SEES

"One thing I do know. I was blind, and now I can see.'" JOHN 9:25

One day Jesus saw a blind man.
"Why was he born blind?" asked Jesus'
followers. "Was it his sins or his parents'
sins?"
"Neither," Jesus answered. "He was born
blind so God's power could be shown in him."

Jesus put mud on the man's eyes and said,
"Go and wash in the Pool of Siloam."
The blind man washed in the water.
He could see!
Several people asked him, "Are you the blind
beggar? How did you get your sight?"

He answered, "Jesus healed me!"
When the Jewish leaders heard his story,
they did not believe it.
They asked his parents if he really had been
born blind.

Again they asked the man, "What happened?"
He answered, "All I know is that once I was
blind, and now I can see!"
The Jewish leaders threw him out of the temple.
Jesus found the man and asked him, "Do you
believe in Me?"
"Yes, Lord, I believe!" the man said.

THE GOOD NEIGHBOR

"'Love the Lord your God. Love him with all your heart, all your soul, all your strength, and all your mind. Also, you must love your neighbor as you love yourself.'" Luke 10:27

A Jewish lawyer asked Jesus, "What must I do to go to heaven?"

"What does God's law say?" asked Jesus.

"Love the Lord with all your heart and your neighbor as yourself," he answered.

"You are right," said Jesus.

"But, who is my neighbor?" asked the lawyer.

Jesus told him a story.
"Once a traveler was attacked by robbers.
They beat him and left him to die in a ditch.
Then a priest passed by. But when he saw the
injured man, he walked by on the other side
of the road," said Jesus.

"Next a temple worker hurried by.
He didn't stop to help, either.
Finally, a foreigner saw the poor man.
He bandaged the man's wounds.
Then he lifted the man out of the ditch and
took him to a safe place."

Jesus asked the lawyer, "Which man was a
good neighbor to the hurting stranger?"
"The man who helped him," said the lawyer.
Jesus said, "Go and do the same thing. Take
care of the hurting people around you."

THE LOST SON

"The son said, 'Father, I have sinned against God and have done wrong to you. I am not good enough to be called your son.'" LUKE 15:21

Jesus told a story about a man with two sons. One son said, "Father, I want my share of your wealth while I'm still young!"
So the father divided his riches. This son took his share and went to a distant land.

He wasted all his money on wicked living.
Soon he was hungry and had nothing to eat.
So he found a job feeding pigs.
He watched the pigs gobble down their food,
and he was so hungry he was willing to
share their meal.

Then the son remembered the good food his father fed the servants. He decided to go home. "I'll tell my father I'm sorry, and I'll ask him to forgive me," he thought.

"Maybe my father will hire me as a servant."

When the son returned home, his father ran
to him and kissed him.
The father said, "My son, you've come home!
 I thought you were dead, but you're alive!"
Then the father had a great party for the lost
son who came home.
Jesus said to His followers, "This is how
God loves the sinner who is sorry."

LAZARUS LIVES!

"Jesus said to her, 'I am the resurrection and the life. He who believes in me will have life even if he dies. And he who lives and believes in me will never die.'" JOHN 11:25, 26

Jesus often stayed at the home of Mary, Martha, and Lazarus. Jesus enjoyed visiting with His friends. Sometimes Mary was so interested in what Jesus was saying that she forgot to do her chores.

But Martha spent her time cooking and cleaning. Once Martha got upset and said, "Lord, don't You care that I'm doing the work alone? Please tell my sister to help me!" Jesus said, "Mary is doing the most important thing. She is listening to Me."

One day the sisters sent a message to Jesus:
"Lazarus is very sick!"
Jesus said to His followers, "This sickness
is so people can see the power of God and
praise Him."
Jesus loved Lazarus, but it was two days
before He went to see His friend.

When Jesus got there, Lazarus had died and
was buried in a cave.
Martha said, "Lord, if You had been here, my
brother wouldn't have died!"
Jesus replied, "He who believes in Me will
have life even if he dies." Mary fell at Jesus'
feet and cried. Jesus felt very sad.

Jesus prayed. Then He said, "Lazarus, come out!" Lazarus walked out of the cave. He was alive again!

Many people saw Jesus raise Lazarus from the dead. From then on, they believed in Jesus.

JESUS BLESSES THE CHILDREN

"Jesus said, 'Let the little children come to me. Don't stop them, because the kingdom of heaven belongs to people who are like these children.'" MATTHEW 19:14

One day Jesus' followers asked Him,
"Who is greatest in the kingdom of heaven?"
Jesus called a small child to His side.
He said, "The one who obeys and trusts Me
like this child is greatest in the Kingdom."

Jesus told His followers, "Children are very
important to God." Then Jesus told a story
to show how much God loves His children.
"A man had one hundred sheep. One sheep
got lost. The man left the other ninety-nine
sheep to search for the lost one."

"He searched everywhere until he found the lost sheep. The man was very happy. He put the sheep on his shoulders and carried it home. In the same way, your heavenly Father does not want any of His children to be lost."

Later, the people brought their children to Jesus so He could pray for them.
Jesus' followers thought He was too busy teaching to bother with babies. But Jesus said, "Let the children come to Me!"
He held the children and blessed them.

TEN HEALING MIRACLES

"When one of them saw that he was healed, he went back to Jesus. He praised God in a loud voice. Then he bowed down at Jesus' feet and thanked him." LUKE *17:15, 16*

On the way to Jerusalem, Jesus met ten men.
Their bodies were covered with ugly sores,
and they were very sad.
They had left their families and friends so
others would not catch their disease.

"Master, please help us!" they called.
Jesus said, "Go and show the priests that
you are healed."
As the men obeyed Jesus, their sores went
away.
All the men were happy they were healed.

One man hurried back to thank Jesus.
He said, "Glory to God, I'm healed!"
"Ten men were healed," said Jesus.
"Where are the other nine?"
Jesus was disappointed that they forgot to
praise God for their healing.
But He was pleased with the thankful man.

MARY ANOINTS JESUS

"Jesus answered, 'Let her alone. It was right for her to save this perfume for today—the day for me to be prepared for burial.'" JOHN 12:7

Jesus returned to Lazarus's house. Lazarus, Mary, and Martha held a dinner to honor Jesus. Martha served the food.
Lazarus ate with Jesus.
And Mary did something special to show Jesus how much she loved Him.

She poured a jar of costly perfume on Jesus'
head and feet. Then she wiped His feet with
her hair.
The smell of sweet perfume filled the room.
Jesus' followers said Mary was foolish to
waste the expensive perfume.
But Jesus was pleased with Mary's gift.

HOSANNA TO THE KING!

"They took branches of palm trees and went out to meet Jesus. They shouted, 'Praise God! God bless the One who comes in the name of the Lord! God bless the King of Israel!'" JOHN 12:13

Jesus stopped outside Jerusalem. He told His followers, "In the next town, you will find a donkey that has never been ridden. Untie the donkey and bring it to Me. Tell anyone who asks that it's for the Master."

The men brought the donkey to Jesus.
Then they laid their coats on the donkey's
back for Jesus to sit on.
Jerusalem was crowded with people for the
Passover Feast. Everyone was filled with
excitement!

A great crowd went out to meet Jesus as He
entered the city of Jerusalem.
The people shouted praises to God for
sending Jesus, the promised King.
They called, "Hosanna! Blessed is the King!"
They waved branches from palm trees and
spread their coats on the road like a carpet.

Loud praises filled the city.
But some of the Jewish leaders did not
believe in Jesus. They said, "Teacher, tell
Your followers to be quiet."
But Jesus said, "If the people don't praise Me,
even the rocks will cry out with joy!"

JESUS IN THE TEMPLE

"They asked Jesus, 'Do you hear the things these children are saying?' Jesus answered, 'Yes. Haven't you read in the Scriptures, "You have taught children and babies to sing praises"?'" MATTHEW 21:16

The next morning, Jesus went into the temple.
He was very upset by what He saw.
The temple workers were cheating the people.
They were making the people pay a high price
to worship at the temple. And the workers
were keeping the money for themselves.

340

Jesus threw out all the greedy people
who were selling things in the temple.
He said, "It says in Scripture, 'My temple
will be called a house of prayer.'
But you have changed God's house
into a place for thieves!"

Then Jesus taught in the temple. He healed
blind and crippled people there.
The children sang praises to Him:
"Hosanna to the Son of David!"
This made the Jewish priests very angry.
They began making a plan to kill Jesus.

THE WIDOW'S GIFT

"'She gave all she had.'" MARK *12:44*

Jesus stood in the temple. He watched
the people bring their offerings to God.
The rich people smiled proudly. They put
large gifts of money in the offering box.

One poor woman dropped two small coins in the box. Jesus told His followers, "This poor widow gave more than the rest. Everyone else has plenty. They gave a little of what they did not need. She needed that money. But she gave all she had."

THE MASTER SERVES HIS FOLLOWERS

"'I did this as an example for you. So you should do as I have done for you. I tell you the truth. A servant is not greater than his master.'"
JOHN *13:15, 16*

Jesus' followers asked Him, "Where do You want to eat the Passover feast?"
Jesus said, "Go into the city. You will find a man carrying a jar of water to a house. Tell the man the Teacher wants to use his house."

Everything happened as Jesus had said.
That evening Jesus and His twelve followers
went to the house. They ate their supper in
the large room upstairs. During the meal,
Jesus poured water into a bowl. Then He
began to wash the followers' feet.

Peter said, "Master, You shouldn't act like a
servant. I don't want You to wash my feet!"
But Jesus said, "If I don't wash you,
you can't be one of My people."
Peter cried, "Lord, please wash my hands
and head, too!"
Jesus taught them how to humbly serve others.

THE LAST MEAL

" 'I give you a new command: Love each other. You must love each other as I have loved you.' " JOHN 13:34

After Jesus washed His followers' feet,
He sat down with them.
Jesus knew it was almost time for Him
to go back to heaven.
He said, "One of you will turn against Me."

The followers were upset.
John asked, "Who will turn against You?"
Jesus dipped a piece of bread into the dish.
He said, "I will give this bread to the wicked
one." Jesus gave the bread to Judas.
Judas quickly left the room.

Jesus knew He would die for the sins of the people. He picked up the bread. He blessed it and broke it.

Then He gave it to the followers to eat. He said, "This bread is My body, given for you. Do this to remember Me."

After they ate, Jesus took the cup.
He thanked God for it.
He said, "This cup is a sign of the new
promise between God and His people.
Drink this. And remember My blood
will cover your sins."

Jesus said, "I will be leaving soon."
The followers felt very sad.
But Jesus cheered them up, "Don't worry.
My Father will give you another Helper.
He will send the Holy Spirit.
And later I will come back to you."

THE JUDAS KISS

"'Father, if it is what you want, then let me not have this cup of suffering. But do what you want, not what I want.'" LUKE 22:42

When the meal was over, Jesus and His followers sang a song.
Then they went to a place to pray.
Jesus warned them, "Tonight you will all leave Me."

"I won't!" said Peter.

Jesus said, "Before morning, you will say
three times that you don't know Me."

Jesus was sad. He told Peter, James, and John,
"Stay awake and pray for strength."

Then Jesus knelt to pray.

An angel from heaven came to comfort Him.

When Jesus finished praying,
His followers were asleep.
"Wake up!" Jesus said. "The time has come!"
Just then, Judas led an angry crowd to Jesus.
They were carrying torches, swords, and clubs.

Judas promised to give Jesus to the Jewish leaders for thirty pieces of silver. He acted like a friend and kissed Jesus. That was how Judas pointed out Jesus to the soldiers.

PETER'S LIE

". . . Jesus had told him: Before the rooster crows you will say . . . you don't know me.'" MATTHEW 26:75

The soldiers grabbed Jesus to arrest Him. Peter took a knife and cut off a man's ear. But Jesus cried, "Stop!" Then He touched the man's ear and healed him.

All the followers were afraid and ran away.
The soldiers took Jesus to the house of the
high priest. Peter followed far behind them.
In the courtyard, a servant girl asked Peter,
"Are you a follower of Jesus?"
Peter said, "No!"

Someone else said, "You were with Jesus!"
Again Peter said, "No, I wasn't!"
Later some people said, "You talk like Jesus."
Peter swore, "I don't know Him."
A rooster crowed, and Peter remembered
Jesus' words. Peter was very sorry.

THE LAMB OF GOD

"But Jesus said nothing. Again the high priest said to Jesus, 'You must swear to this. I command you by the power of the living God to tell us the truth. Tell us, are you the Christ . . . ?'" MATTHEW 26:63

The lawyers told people to lie about Jesus to the Jewish court. When these people lied, Jesus said nothing.
Then the priest asked, "Are You God's Son?" Jesus said, "I am."

His answer made the people angry.
They spit on Him and slapped His face.
Then the Jewish leaders took Jesus before
Pilate, the Roman governor.
They told Pilate, "He claims to be a king!"

Pilate asked Jesus, "Are You a king?"
Jesus answered, "Yes. My kingdom is in
heaven." Pilate found nothing wrong with
Jesus. Pilate told the people that he was
going to release Jesus.

But the angry people yelled, "Kill Him!
Kill Him on a cross! Free the prisoner
Barabbas instead."
Pilate listened to the people.
He let Barabbas, the murderer, go free.
And he said Jesus must die on a cross.

THE CROSS

"Jesus cried out in a loud voice, 'Father, I give you my life.' After Jesus said this, he died." LUKE 23:46

The Roman soldiers beat Jesus. They dressed Him like a king to make fun of Him. Then they made Him carry a cross through the city.

The cross was very heavy. So the soldiers forced a man in the crowd to help Jesus carry it. Finally, they came to a place called Golgotha. There, the soldiers nailed Jesus' hands and feet to the cross.

Two criminals were nailed on crosses next
to Jesus. Jesus' followers were sad and cried.
But many people laughed at Him.
Jesus said, "Father, forgive them.
They don't know what they are doing."

When Jesus died, the sky turned black and
the earth shook. The soldiers were afraid.
They said, "He really *was* the Son of God!"
Jesus' body was laid in a tomb.
A large stone was rolled across the entrance
to the tomb.

HE'S ALIVE!

" 'Go quickly and tell his followers. Say to them: 'Jesus has risen from death.' " MATTHEW 28:7

On Sunday morning, Mary Magdalene
and some other women went to the tomb.
Just then there was an earthquake.
An angel came down from heaven and rolled
away the stone from the tomb.

The angel sat on the stone.
The soldiers guarding the tomb shook
with fear and became like dead men.
The angel told the women, "Don't be afraid. I
know you are looking for Jesus. But He is not
here. He is risen, as He said He would."

Then the angel said, "Go quickly. Tell
His followers Jesus has risen from death!"
The women hurried away. They were afraid
but happy. They ran to tell Jesus' followers
what had happened.

Suddenly Jesus stood before them.
The women fell down at His feet and
worshiped Him.
"Don't be afraid," Jesus said. "Tell My brothers
to go to Galilee. They will see Me there."

A MEALTIME MIRACLE

"While the two followers were telling this, Jesus himself stood among those gathered. He said to them, 'Peace be with you.'" LUKE 24:36

Jesus appeared to Peter, alone.
Then Peter told the followers,
"The Lord has really risen!" Later, eleven of
Jesus' followers were eating together.
Suddenly Jesus appeared to them, too.

The followers were very afraid.
They thought they were seeing a ghost.
But Jesus said, "Why do you doubt?
It is I Myself! See My hands and feet?"
They saw the scars on His hands and feet,
and they believed.

The followers were amazed and happy.
Jesus asked, "Do you have any food here?"
They gave Jesus some cooked fish to eat.
Jesus told them, "The Scripture says
the Messiah would be killed and would rise
from death on the third day."

Jesus said, "You have seen these things happen, just as the prophets said they would. Now go into all the world and tell the Good News. Tell people their sins will be forgiven when they turn to Me."

JESUS GOES HOME

" 'You saw Jesus taken away from you into heaven. He will come back in the same way you saw him go.' " ACTS 1:11

Jesus led His followers to a mountain outside the city.
He said, "In a few days, you will be baptized in the Holy Spirit. Don't leave Jerusalem until you receive this promise."

He said, "The Holy Spirit will give you power
to be My witnesses in all the world."
Jesus blessed them.
The followers worshiped Jesus.
Then He went up into the sky.

They watched Jesus being carried into heaven
in a cloud. Suddenly two angels appeared.
They said, "Jesus will come again in the
same way you saw Him go!"

TONGUES OF FIRE

"Joel the prophet wrote . . . 'God says: I will give my Spirit freely to all kinds of people.'" Acts 2:16–17

Each day Jesus' followers met together to pray. The believers were waiting for their promise from God.

During this time, the believers gathered
to celebrate Pentecost.
This was the Jewish Harvest Festival.
Suddenly a noise came from heaven.
It sounded like a strong wind blowing,
and it filled the whole house.

It looked like a tongue of fire
rested on the head of each believer.
The believers were all filled with the Holy
Spirit, and they began to speak in different
languages!

PEOPLE OF POWER

"'The Holy Spirit will come to you. Then you will receive power. You will be my witnesses.'" ACTS 1:8

Jewish people from every country were in Jerusalem for Pentecost.
They were surprised.
"How can this be?" they said. "We hear these believers speaking in our own languages about the great things God has done!"

Peter stood up and boldly told the people the good news about Jesus. "Be baptized in the name of Jesus Christ," Peter said. "Let Jesus forgive you and save you from sin! Then you will receive the Holy Spirit, too!"

The people who believed what Peter said were baptized.
About 3,000 people were added to the number of believers that day.

The believers spent much of their time together. They worshiped God in the temple each day. They also met in their homes to break bread and pray. They gave to the poor. And God blessed them with more new believers.

As the believers shared with each other, their
hearts were filled with joy. They praised God,
and God gave them everything they needed.
With great power, these followers
told people about Jesus.

A CRIPPLED MAN IS HEALED

"'By the power of Jesus Christ from Nazareth—stand up and walk!'"
ACTS 3:6

The followers did many miracles. One day,
Peter and John went to the temple to pray.
At the temple gate sat a crippled beggar.
The man asked Peter and John for money.

Peter said, "I don't have any money. But I can give you something else. By the power of Jesus—stand up and walk!"
The man jumped up.
He walked into the temple praising God.
The people were amazed.
Peter and John began preaching to them.

CAN'T STOP TALKING

"We cannot keep quiet. We must speak about what we have seen and heard." ACTS 4:20

When the Jewish leaders heard that the crippled man could walk, they were very upset.
They asked Peter and John, "By what power did you do this miracle?"
Peter and John told them about Jesus.

389

The Jewish leaders saw that
Peter and John were not afraid.
The leaders knew then that these two men
had been with Jesus.
So they warned Peter and John not to teach
about Jesus anymore.

Peter and John said bravely,
"We can't stop talking about Jesus!
We won't stop praising His name!"
These two men had received power
from the Holy Spirit. And they would never
be the same.

SIGNS AND WONDERS

"'Help us to be brave by showing us your power; make sick people well, give proofs, and make miracles happen.'" Acts 4:30

The Jewish leaders tried to scare
the followers again. But the believers kept
speaking boldly in Jesus' name.
Crowds came to the city with their sick.
And all the people were healed.

The Jewish leaders were jealous.
They put Jesus' followers in jail.
But that night an angel opened the prison
doors. The next day the soldiers found Jesus'
followers preaching in the temple again.
The soldiers took them to the high priest.

The angry priest said, "We warned you not to talk about Jesus anymore!"
Peter said, "We must obey God, not men."
The Jewish leaders had Jesus' followers whipped. But the followers were glad to suffer for Jesus.

STEPHEN

"Stephen continued speaking: '. . . You have not given your hearts to God! You won't listen to him! You are always against what the Holy Spirit is trying to tell you.'" ACTS 7:51

Stephen helped the followers serve food to the poor people.
He was filled with the Holy Spirit.
God gave Stephen the power to do great miracles among the people.

The Jewish leaders were against Stephen.
They tried to argue with him.
But the Spirit gave him great wisdom.
And the Jewish leaders could not fight him.
So the leaders secretly paid some men to lie
about Stephen.

Many people believed the lies. Some of them
grabbed Stephen and took him to the
high priest.
The priest said, "Are these things true?"
Then Stephen began preaching about Jesus.
"Look!" Stephen pointed to the sky. "I see
heaven open. Jesus is standing next to God!"

This made some of the Jewish leaders mad.
They took Stephen out of the city
and threw stones at him.
Stephen fell to his knees and cried,
"Lord, forgive them!"
And then he died.

Some of the Jewish leaders tried to
kill all the believers in Jerusalem.
Many people escaped from harm by
quickly moving to other cities.
These believers took the good news of Jesus
with them wherever they went.

THE MAGICIAN

"And everywhere they were scattered, they told people the Good News."
ACTS 8:4

A believer named Philip went to Samaria to preach about Jesus. He healed the weak and crippled people there.
Many of the people had evil spirits in them. But Philip made the evil spirits go away.

In Samaria a magician named Simon
amazed people with his magic tricks.
His friends said he had "the Great Power."
Philip told Simon and his friends
about the power of Jesus.

They saw the miracles Philip did, and they
believed the good news of Jesus. Philip
baptized the new believers. Later, Peter and
John came to Samaria. They saw that the
new believers had not yet received the Holy
Spirit. Peter and John placed their hands on
the people and prayed for them.

The new believers received the Holy Spirit. When Simon saw this, he offered Peter money for this power. Peter said, "You're full of jealousy and sin! You can't buy God's gift!" Simon said, "Please pray that the Lord will forgive me." So Peter and John prayed for Simon.

PHILIP BAPTIZES A RICH MAN

"Both Philip and the officer went down into the water, and Philip baptized him." ACTS 8:38

An angel told Philip to go to the desert road that leads to Gaza from Jerusalem.
On the road, Philip saw an important officer from Ethiopia.
The man was sitting in his chariot, reading Scripture.

The Spirit told Philip, "Go to the chariot!"
So Philip ran up to the side of the chariot.
And he asked the man, "Do you understand
what you are reading?"
The man said, "I need someone to explain
it to me!"
Philip gladly explained God's Word, and
told the man about Jesus.
The man believed and was baptized.

SAUL SEES THE LIGHT

"The Lord Jesus sent me. He is the one you saw on the road on your way here." ACTS 9:17

In Jerusalem, a Jewish leader called Saul tried to frighten the followers of Jesus. Saul went from house to house, searching for believers. When he found followers of Jesus, he threw them in jail.

One day Saul was on his way to the city of
Damascus. He was going there to look for
believers, too.
Suddenly a bright light from heaven blinded
him. He fell to the ground.
A voice from heaven said, "Saul, why are you
doing things against Me?"

Saul asked, "Who are You, Lord?"
"I am Jesus!" the voice answered. "I am the
One you are trying to hurt!"
Then Jesus told Saul to go to Damascus
and wait for someone to help him. Saul
opened his eyes, but he could not see!

The men traveling with Saul heard the voice, too. But they saw no one!
The men took Saul by the hand and led him into the city. For three days, Saul could not see, and he did not drink or eat.

Ananias, a follower of Jesus, lived in Damascus. The Lord spoke to Ananias in a vision. "Quickly, go to Straight Street. Find the house of Judas. Ask for Saul. Tell him about Me!"

Ananias was afraid because he had heard that Saul hated all believers.

Still, Ananias obeyed the Lord. He found Saul
praying in the house of Judas. He put
his hands on Saul's eyes. Ananias said,
"Saul, the Lord Jesus sent me to you. Jesus
wants you to see again and be filled with the
Holy Spirit!" At once Saul could see!

PAUL IN A BASKET

"Soon he began to preach about Jesus in the synagogues, saying, 'Jesus is the Son of God!'" Acts 9:20

Saul was happy to learn the truth about Jesus. Now he knew Jesus really was the promised Son of God!
And he began telling other people about the Good News.

Saul became known as Paul, the preacher.
He was a changed man!
The Jewish leaders planned to kill Paul.
But some followers helped Paul escape
by lowering him over the city wall in a
basket.

RISE AND BE HEALED!

". . . He turned to the body and said, 'Tabitha, stand up!' She opened her eyes, and . . . sat up." ACTS 9:40

Peter preached in Joppa.
A woman named Tabitha lived there.
She always helped the poor.
And the people loved her dearly.
Suddenly Tabitha became sick and died.
The believers quickly sent for Peter.

When Peter got there, some poor widows
were standing around the dead body
crying.
"Look at our beautiful clothes," the women
cried. "Tabitha made them for us."
Then Peter told everyone to leave the room.
He prayed for Tabitha. She opened her eyes
and sat up!

THE HOLY SPIRIT IS FOR EVERYONE

"God accepts anyone who worships him and does what is right. It is not important what country a person comes from." Acts 10:35

A soldier named Cornelius loved God. He prayed daily and gave money to poor people. One day he saw a vision. An angel said, "God is pleased with your gifts. He hears your prayers. I will bring Peter to your house, and he will preach to you."

416

Peter also had a strange vision.
In it the Holy Spirit told him to eat things
forbidden by Jewish law! Then the Spirit told
him that some men were looking for him.
The Spirit said, "Go with these men to their
house. Preach to them. I have sent them."

Peter obeyed the Holy Spirit.
He went with the men. He told Cornelius
and his family about Jesus. While they were
listening, the Holy Spirit came into their
hearts. They began speaking in languages
they had not learned! Peter was amazed.

Now Peter understood his vision.
The Holy Spirit is for people from every
country. The good news of Jesus is not just
for Jewish people! Peter baptized the new
believers. Then he ate with his new friends.

A MISSION

"They laid their hands on Barnabas and Saul and sent them out."
ACTS 13:3

One day Paul was worshiping the Lord with a group of believers. Some of these people were prophets. The Holy Spirit said to them, "I have chosen Paul and the believer Barnabas to do a special job."

The people prayed. They placed their hands
on Paul and Barnabas. The believers
blessed them.
Then they sent Paul and Barnabas to preach
the Good News in other lands.

LIGHT AND DARKNESS

"He looked straight at Elymas and said, '. . . You are full of evil tricks. . . . You are always trying to change the Lord's truth into lies! Now the Lord will touch you, and you will be blind.'" ACTS 13:9–11

In Paphos, the governor wanted to hear the message of God. Paul and Barnabas preached to him.
But a false prophet named Elymas didn't want the governor to hear God's Word.

Elymas tried to keep the governor from
believing in Jesus. Paul told Elymas,
"The Lord will make you blind for trying to
change His truth into lies!"
Suddenly Elymas could not see.
The governor saw this miracle and believed.

THE FORTUNE-TELLER

"'These men are servants of the Most High God! They are telling you how you can be saved!'" ACTS 16:17

One day Paul and his friend Silas were going
to a prayer meeting near the river.
They met a slave girl who had an evil spirit.
She began to shout at them.
She wouldn't keep quiet.

The girl was a fortune-teller. She told people
what was going to happen to them. She
made lots of money for her owners. For
many days she followed Paul and Silas.
Again and again she shouted, "These men
are servants of the Most High God!"

Finally Paul said, "By the power of
Jesus Christ, I tell you to come out of her!"
At once, the evil spirit came out of the girl.
She became calm and quiet.
But her owners were very angry. They
couldn't use her to make money anymore.

PRAISES FROM PRISON

". . . 'Believe in the Lord Jesus and you will be saved—you and all the people in your house.'" Acts *16:31*

Paul and Silas were beaten and
thrown into prison.
About midnight, they were praying
and singing songs to God.
The other prisoners were listening to them.

Suddenly an earthquake shook the jail.
The doors of the prison broke open.
The prisoners' chains fell off!
The jail guard woke up with a jolt.
He thought all his prisoners had escaped.
The jailer was very upset. He reached for
his sword to kill himself.

Paul shouted, "Don't worry! We're here."
The jailer shook with fear and fell down
before Paul and Silas.
"What must I do to be saved?" he asked.
They said, "Believe in the Lord Jesus.
Then you and your family will be saved!"

The jailer took Paul and Silas home with
him. He washed their wounds and gave them
food to eat. Then Paul and Silas told the
jailer and his family about Jesus.
The jailer's family was baptized.
They were filled with joy!

PAUL IS ARRESTED

"I have fought the good fight. I have finished the race. I have kept the faith." 2 Timothy 4:7

Paul preached about Jesus all his life. When Paul grew old, he was arrested again for being a follower of Jesus. Soldiers took Paul to Rome in chains. He spent the rest of his life in jail. But even in prison, he preached about Jesus.

LETTERS FROM PRISON

"I can do all things through Christ because he gives me strength."
Philippians 4:13

Paul wrote many letters to cheer up
the believers he had met in his travels. In the
letters he told his friends, "Give thanks
whatever happens. Do not stop the work of
the Holy Spirit!"

"Learn the Word of God," Paul's letters said.
"Pray in the Spirit at all times.
Remember to keep the faith.
And never give up!"

433

THE CITY OF GOD

"Hallelujah! Our Lord God rules. He is the All-Powerful."
REVELATION 19:6

One day John was worshiping God.
 He heard a loud voice that said,
"I am the start and the finish!"
Jesus appeared, dressed in a white robe.
 He was shining like a bright light.
John fell at His feet in fear.

Jesus said, "Do not be afraid. I am going to show you things no man has ever seen. Write these things in a book, and send it to the churches." The power of the Spirit carried John to a high mountain. He saw the golden city of heaven. All the people who love Jesus live there forever with God.

There is no crying or dying in the city of God.
There is no more sickness or sadness.
The Devil will be destroyed forever.
Everyone there is singing and serving God.
The city does not need sunshine. God's
glory is bright enough light for everyone to see.

Then John saw God's throne.
A rainbow was over the throne.
A beautiful river that looked like glass lay
before it. Next to God's throne were angels
saying, "Holy, holy, holy is the Lord."
Many people were worshiping at God's feet.

CHRIST'S RETURN

"'Listen! I am coming soon! He who obeys the words of prophecy in this book will be happy.'" REVELATION *22:7*

The sky opened. And John saw Jesus sitting on a white horse.

Jesus said, "I am coming to take My children to heaven with Me. I will punish people who do not love Me. I will bless the people who obey Me. Be ready, for I am coming soon!"

Jesus Loves Me
DEVOTIONAL

Angela Abraham and Ken Abraham

Illustrations by Terry Anderson and Kathleen Dunne

www.tommynelson.com

A Division of Thomas Nelson, Inc.
www.ThomasNelson.com

THE LORD'S PRAYER

"Our Father in heaven,

we pray that your name will always be
    kept holy.

We pray that your kingdom will come.

We pray that what you want will be done,
    here on earth as it is in heaven.

Give us the food we need for each day.

Forgive the sins we have done,
    just as we have forgiven those who did
    wrong to us.

Do not cause us to be tested; but save us
    from the Evil One."

—MATTHEW 6:9–13

God wants me to pray, praise, and thank Him
no matter how I feel . . . what I do . . .
where I go . . . or who I'm with.

CONTENTS

HOW I FEEL

"Praise the Lord. He heard my prayer for help. The Lord is my strength and shield. I trust him, and he helps me. I am very happy. And I praise him with my song." —PSALM 28:6–7

WHAT I DO

"Lord, teach me your ways. Guide me to do what is right. . . ." —PSALM 27:11

WHERE I GO

"Lord . . . You know all about me. You know where I go and where I lie down. You know well everything I do. Your knowledge is amazing to me. It is more than I can understand." —PSALM 139:1, 3, 6

WHO I AM WITH

"The Lord is great. He is worthy of our praise. . . . The Lord will keep his promises. With love he takes care of all he has made. . . . The Lord is close to everyone who prays to him." —PSALM 145:3, 13, 18

INDEX

HOW TO USE THIS BOOK

Dear Parents,

In writing this devotional for little ones, we have tried to create an exciting way for children ages three to eight to celebrate God's love and care for them every day. We have chosen a variety of songs, Bible stories, poems, activities, and prayers to show children *how to praise God no matter how they feel, where they go, what they do, or who they are with.*

Each chapter is divided into five sections: **Praise, Prayer, Promise, People in the Bible,** and **Pleasing God.**

First is the **Praise** section. Starting your time together with praise will help your child learn to keep his or her gaze on God instead of on the gifts he or she hopes to get from Him. You and your child can explore various ways of praising God.

Sometimes you will praise Him through a song, sometimes with a poem, or a prayer. At times your praise will be noisy as you clap your hands, march, play homemade instruments, and shout. At other times, you will simply be still and know that He is our almighty God. Can you imagine what it does to the heart of our heavenly Father to hear the voices of our children giving Him praise?

Next, you will find suggestions for talking to God in **Prayer**. These prayers include prayer poems, prayers from the Bible, and modern-day prayers. This section will help children know they can pray anytime, anywhere, in groups, or alone. Their prayers can be aloud or silent, long or short.

Children will learn to talk to God about anything . . . and everything! They will learn to talk to God when they are happy, sad, lonely, afraid, or angry, and they will tell God how they feel. They will thank Him for friends, family, flowers, and fun times. They will learn that whatever they do or wherever they go, they can talk to God. They can pray on the way to school or on a ball field, just as easily as they can pray at church. Children will learn that prayer is more than reciting words to God. It is sharing with Him from the heart. It is listening for His voice and obeying what He says.

The third section in each chapter is a Bible **Promise**. One way God speaks to us is through His Word. You may want your child to memorize these encouraging verses from Scripture. Take some time each day to think about these truths. This will help your child understand what it means to "wait upon the Lord" and to watch and listen for answers to their prayers.

Fourth is a section describing **People in the Bible**. This is a Bible story illustrating the main point in each chapter. It is also the passage of Scripture on which the truth being emphasized is based. Children will learn to obey God's Word by following the examples of the people in the Bible.

Each chapter ends with a **Pleasing God** section which includes fun activities such as making a *thankful necklace* or a *prayer album*, or doing a simple finger play or action rhyme. These practical applications will help bring the Bible truths to life in an easy-to-remember way.

It is our hope that this book will lay a foundation in tender, young hearts for a growing, thriving relationship with God. As you learn to praise God with your child, you too will become encouraged! As you learn to pray together, your faith in God will become stronger. Remember God has promised to bless you as you praise Him. And God always keeps His promises!

ANGELA ABRAHAM AND KEN ABRAHAM

I PRAISE GOD FOR HIS LOVE

What is the best gift you've ever been given? Have you ever thought of Jesus as a gift? God has! God showed His love for you by sending Jesus to be your Savior.

How can you show God you are thankful for His gift of love?

Praise

Sing this chorus to the tune of "Ring Around the Rosy."

God's Love Is Amazing

God's love is amazing.
Children thank and praise Him,
Love Him, serve Him—
Let's all bow down.

Ask a parent, brother, sister, or friend to sing this chorus with you. "Praisers" form a circle holding hands. As you sing the chorus, circle to the left (clockwise). At the end of the song, drop your hands and kneel down. Bow your head and fold your hands as though you are praying.

Prayer

Father, We Thank Thee

Father, we thank Thee for the night,
And for the pleasant morning light,
For rest and food and loving care,
And all that makes the world so fair.

Help us to do the things we should,
To be to others kind and good,
In all we do and all we say,
To grow more loving every day.

—AUTHOR UNKNOWN

Promise

". . . we should love each other, because love comes from God. The person who loves has become God's child and knows God. Whoever does not love does not know God, because God is love."

—1 JOHN 4:7–8

People in the Bible

Mary and Martha held a dinner to honor Jesus. Martha served the food. Lazarus ate with Jesus.

Mary did something special to show Jesus how much she loved Him. Mary knew that Jesus was God's holy Son.

Mary poured a jar of costly perfume on Jesus' head and feet. Then she wiped His feet with her hair. The smell of sweet perfume filled the room.

3

Jesus' followers said Mary was foolish to waste the expensive perfume. They complained, "The perfume should be sold and the money given to the poor."

Jesus' followers did not understand Mary's actions. But Jesus was pleased with Mary's gift of love. "Leave her alone," said Jesus. "Mary did the right thing."

Mary had given praise to God by her act of kindness.

Pleasing God

Mary showed her love for Jesus by giving Him the best gift she had. Mary was thankful for Jesus, her Savior. She praised God for His gift of love.

How can you show Jesus you love Him?

How can you share God's love with others?

Try making a *heart filled with love.* Draw a big, red heart on white construction paper. Draw a picture of Jesus inside the heart. Cut out the heart. Give your heart to someone you love. Remember to tell him or her about God's gift of love!

5

I PRAISE GOD WHEN I AM HAPPY

Let's think some happy thoughts together.

I feel happy when I _____.

I can make others happy when I _____.

How can you make God happy?

Praise

Sing this chorus to the tune of "The More We Get Together."

Praise God When I Am Happy

Praise God when I am happy, I'm happy, I'm happy.
Praise God when I am happy. I thank God today.
I share with my brother. We help one another.
Praise God when I am happy. I thank God this way.

Praise God when I'm not happy, not happy, not happy.
Praise God when I'm not happy. I thank God anyway.
I listen to my father. I obey my mother.
Praise God when I'm not happy. I thank Him always!

6

Prayer

Dear Jesus,
Thank You for everything that makes me smile, like chocolate-chip
cookies, ice cream, and jelly beans. Thank You for happy thoughts of
birthday parties, bunny rabbits, and baseball. I thank You for happy
times on bikes, vacations, and picnics. Most of all, I thank You for
friends to laugh with and family to love!

Love,
Me

Promise

"Happy are the people who know how to praise you.
Lord, let them live in the light of your presence.
In your name they rejoice all the time. They praise your goodness."

—PSALM 89:15–16

People in the Bible

David loved the Lord with all his heart. He happily wrote
many songs of praise while caring for his sheep. He sang,
"Lord, Your name is the most wonderful name in all the
earth. Even children and babies sing praises to You."

David wrote, "Children, come and listen to me. I will teach you to worship the Lord." He sang, "Every good thing I have comes from the Lord."

David said, "I praise the Lord at all times. His praise is always on my lips."

Pleasing God

Would you like to do something that will make someone smile?

Ask your mother if you can help her bake a batch of cutout cookies. Yum! Yum! Remember to thank God before eating, and don't forget to share!

Recipe:

1 cup butter

1 3/4 cup sugar

2 eggs

1 cup sour cream

1/2 teaspoon vanilla

1/2 teaspoon salt

1 teaspoon baking soda

1 teaspoon baking powder

4 1/2 cups flour

Cream the butter and sugar together; add the eggs, sour cream, and vanilla. Beat until creamy. Combine the salt, soda, baking powder, and flour. Slowly add dry mixture to creamy mixture, stirring after each addition. Chill the dough. Roll out dough and cut into desired shapes with a cookie cutter. Bake at 350 degrees for approximately ten minutes.

A PRAYER WHEN I FEEL SAD

What makes you feel sad? Did you know Jesus gets disappointed, too? What do you think might make Jesus sad?

Praise

Say the words from Psalm 34:1–2 aloud, with the following actions.

"*I* (point to yourself) *will praise the Lord* (raise hands heavenward) *at all times. His praise is always on my lips* (point to lips). *My whole being* (cross hands over your heart) *praises the Lord* (raise hands heavenward)."

11

Prayer

Dear Lord,
Open up a window,
*   in the cellar of my soul.*
Let me walk in sunshine,
*   wherever I may go.*
Lift my thoughts toward heaven
*   and gently let me know.*
That You are walking with me
*   wherever I may go.*
In Jesus' Name, amen.

Promise

"Always be happy. Never stop praying.
Give thanks whatever happens.
That is what God wants for you in Christ Jesus."

—1 THESSALONIANS 5:16–18

12

People in the Bible

On the way to Jerusalem, Jesus met ten men. Their bodies were covered with ugly sores, and they were very sad. They had left their families and friends so others would not catch their disease.

"Master, please help us!" they called.

Jesus said, "Go and show the priests that you are healed."

As the men obeyed Jesus, their sores went away.

13

All the men were happy they were healed. One man hurried back to thank Jesus.

He said, "Glory to God! I'm healed!"

"Ten men were healed," said Jesus. "Where are the other nine?"

Jesus was disappointed that they forgot to praise God for their healing. But He was pleased with the thankful man.

Pleasing God

If you are disappointed about something, try making a *thankful necklace* out of a paper chain.

List several things you are thankful for—your family, food, home, and other things. Draw a picture of each thing you are thankful for on a strip of paper. Glue the ends together, making a circle. Thread the next strip of paper through the circle and glue the ends together, making another circle. Continue adding paper circles until your necklace is large enough to fit over your head.

Wear your *thankful necklace* whenever you feel disappointed. It will help you remember all the things you have to be thankful for!

A PROMISE WHEN I FEEL LONELY

Do you ever feel lonely? Do you know it is possible to be alone, yet not lonely? Jesus is with you all the time, even when no one else is around!

Praise

I would like to play with someone today,
But I am alone with no friends of my own.
Lord, let me reach for Your hand, again,
When I feel lonely and need a friend.
And thank You for listening to my prayer,
It always helps me to know that You care!

Angela Abraham / copyright © 1995 by House of Abraham

16

Prayer

Dear Jesus,
You are the only One who knows I'm crying. I'm afraid of being by
myself. I feel all alone. I'm afraid of strangers. Lord, will You protect
me? Please send me a friend. And help me to remember that You are
my best Friend. Thank You for never leaving me! Amen.

Promise

". . . God has said, 'I will never leave you; I will never forget you.' So
we can feel sure and say, 'I will not be afraid because the Lord is my
helper.'"

—*Hebrews 13:5–6*

17

People in the Bible

Elijah came to Mount Sinai, the mountain of God. The Lord
said, "Stand in front of Me. I will pass by you." A great
wind swept by Elijah, but the Lord was not in it. Elijah saw
an earthquake, but the Lord was not in it. A fire passed by,
too, but the Lord was not in it either.

After the fire, Elijah heard a soft voice. He knew it was the voice of the Lord. "Why are you running, Elijah?" the Lord asked him.

"I feel afraid and alone," Elijah said. The Lord said, "Go pour holy oil on Elisha. He will be your helper and friend."

Pleasing God

Can you think of someone who may be lonely right now?

____A friend who has moved away   ____A grandma

____A neighbor   ____A grandpa

The best way to have a friend is to be a friend. How can you be a friend to someone who is lonely?

____Call him or her on the phone.   ____Send him or her a card.

____Write the person a letter.   ____Pray for that person.

The next time you are feeling lonely, talk to your best Friend, Jesus. Ask Him how you can help someone else who may be feeling lonely.

HOW TO PRAY WHEN I AM ANGRY

Have you been angry today? How do you think God feels when you get angry?

Praise

Sing the following song to the tune of "If You're Happy."

> *If you're angry and you know it, stomp your feet*
> (frown; stomp your feet).
> *If you're angry and you know it, stomp your feet*
> (frown; stomp your feet).
> *If you're angry and you know it, then your life will really*
> *show it.*
> *If you're angry and you know it, stomp your feet*
> (frown; stomp your feet).
>
> *If you're happy and you know it, clap your hands*
> (smile; clap your hands).
> *If you're happy and you know it, clap your hands*
> (smile; clap your hands).
> *If you're happy and you know it, then your life will really*
> *show it.*
> *If you're happy and you know it, clap your hands*
> (smile; clap your hands).

Prayer

Dear Lord,

*I know it makes You sad when I get real mad
and start to say things that are bad.*

*Please forgive me today;
Please help me to say
things in a much nicer way.*

In Jesus' Name, amen.

Promise

*"Do not be bitter or angry or mad. . . . You are God's children whom
he loves. So try to be like God. Live a life of love."*

—EPHESIANS 4:31; 5:1–2

People in the Bible

One day Cain and Abel were worshiping God. They each brought God a gift. Abel's gift was good. But Cain's gift was selfish.

Cain was angry that God did not accept his offering. Cain wanted to kill Abel.

"Your heart is angry," God said. "Do good, and I will accept you."

Cain did not obey God. Cain hit Abel and killed him.

"Where is your brother?" God asked.

Cain yelled, "I don't know. Is it my job to take care of him?"

God said, "I see what you did to your brother. You will be punished for the terrible way you treated him."

God told Cain, "Your heart is evil, so you cannot stay in My presence." Cain roamed the earth without God.

Pleasing God

How did God punish Cain?

How do you think that made Cain feel?

When you get angry, ask Jesus to forgive you. He will make your heart clean.

Why is the boy in this picture so happy now? Next time you take a bath, notice how good it feels to be clean.

Next time you get angry, try blowing soap bubbles. This will remind you to keep your heart clean!

25

HELP ME WHEN I AM AFRAID

Can you name a time when you were afraid?

1. Going to the doctor   3. Being alone

2. First day of school   4. Other . . .

Did you pray? What happened?

Praise

Whisper a Prayer

Traditional   Arr. Allan Koppelberger

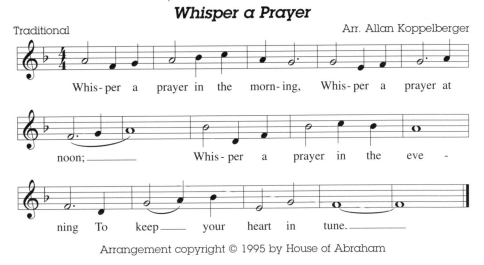

Whis-per a prayer in the morn-ing, Whis-per a prayer at

noon; _____ Whis-per a prayer in the eve -

ning To keep ____ your heart in tune. _____

Arrangement copyright © 1995 by House of Abraham

26

Prayer

Dear Lord,

I hear thunder crash, and I see lightning flash,
'til I'm scared to open my eyes.

Father, would You please help me by
pushing away these frightening clouds
on this dark, dreary day?

Take away my fear and doubt,
lift up my heart, I pray.

In Jesus' Name, amen.

Promise

"So don't worry, because I am with you. Don't be afraid, because I am
your God. I will make you strong and will help you. I will support you
with my right hand that saves you."

—ISAIAH 41:10

27

People in the Bible

Esther was the queen in Persia. No one in the palace knew Esther was Jewish. "Keep it secret," said Esther's Cousin Mordecai. Esther always listened to his wise advice.

Haman, the king's officer, hated Mordecai, the Jew. He made an evil plan to get rid of him. He tricked the king into signing a law that called for all Jewish people living in the land to be killed.

Mordecai asked Esther to talk to the king.

Esther was frightened. She said, "There is a law that forbids me from going to the king without being invited. I could be punished."

Mordecai said, "God may have let you be chosen queen for just such a time as this. Please help your people."

Esther prayed that she would not be afraid. The Lord helped Esther. She boldly went to see the king. The king loved Esther and listened to her. The king punished Haman for his hatred of Mordecai. And God used Esther to save her people!

Pleasing God

Are you afraid of something or someone?

Would you like to have courage like Esther?

God will help you when you trust Him.

List several of your fears on a piece of paper. You may want to draw pictures to show the things you are afraid of.

Now tear the paper into as many pieces as you can. Then throw all the pieces into the garbage. Thank Jesus for taking away all of your fears.

A PROMISE WHEN I AM SICK

Where can you go for help when you are sick?

We thank God for hospitals, doctors, and medicine.

But remember, Jesus is the One who really makes us feel better. Always ask Him for His help.

Praise

Read this prayer from Jeremiah 17:14 aloud.

> *"Lord, heal me, and I will truly be healed.*
> *Save me, and I will truly be saved.*
> *Lord, you are the one I praise."*

31

Prayer

Dear Jesus,
When I feel bad, sick, or tired, I will trust You.
Soothe all my aches, and take away the pain. Help me to rest and feel
better. Please help my family and friends not to worry. Bless everyone
who is praying for me. Thank You, Jesus, for healing me! Amen.

Promise

"The Lord will give him strength when he is sick.
The Lord will make him well again."

—PSALM 41:3

People in the Bible

Peter preached in Joppa. A woman named Tabitha lived there. She always helped the poor. And the people loved her dearly. Suddenly Tabitha became sick and died! The believers quickly sent for Peter.

When Peter arrived all the poor widows were crying. The women were sad because their friend had died. They pointed to the beautiful clothes Tabitha had given them. "Look at what Tabitha made for us," the women said.

Peter kneeled beside Tabitha. He prayed for her, "Tabitha, rise and be healed!"

She opened her eyes! Then Peter held Tabitha's hand and helped her up. Peter called the widows into the room. They were surprised to find Tabitha sitting up. The widows were happy their dear friend was alive.

Many people in Joppa believed in the Lord when they learned about this miracle.

Pleasing God

When Peter prayed for Tabitha, she was made well. Can you think of someone who might not be feeling well? Why not pray for that person right now?

The next time you are sick, make a list of five things you enjoy doing when you feel well. Draw pictures of yourself doing your favorite things. Remember to thank God for making you well.

Draw a picture or card for someone who is sick.

HOW TO PRAY WHEN I AM WORRIED

What do you worry about? God wants to take care of you.
He promises to give you everything you need.

Praise

Cast Your Cares

Angela Abraham

Angela Abraham
Arr. Allan Koppelberger

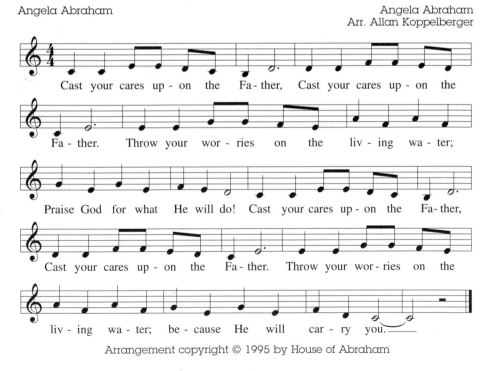

Cast your cares up - on the Fa - ther, Cast your cares up - on the

Fa - ther. Throw your wor - ries on the liv - ing wa - ter;

Praise God for what He will do! Cast your cares up - on the Fa - ther,

Cast your cares up - on the Fa - ther. Throw your wor - ries on the

liv - ing wa - ter; be - cause He will car - ry you.

Arrangement copyright © 1995 by House of Abraham

Prayer

Dear Jesus,
I'm worried about doing something I've never done before. I get
scared about going to new places. I'm afraid of being different than
the other children. If someone asks me a question, help me to know
the answer. If I don't understand something, please make me brave
enough to ask for help. Lord, You give me wisdom and courage.
Thank You for giving me everything I need. Amen.

Promises

"My God will use his wonderful riches in Christ Jesus to give you
everything you need."

—PHILIPPIANS *4:19*

People in the Bible

One day Jesus sat on a hillside and taught His followers.
"See the birds in the sky?" He said. "Your heavenly Father
feeds them. God helps the lovely flowers to grow, too. If God
cares about the birds and flowers, you can trust Him to take
care of you, too!"

Pleasing God

Most of the things we worry about never happen. It pleases God when we stop worrying and start trusting Him. Talk to your heavenly Father. He will take care of you.

The birds don't worry. And the flowers don't fret. So why should you? Scatter some birdseed or bread crumbs outside. Watch how the birds eat the food you have given them. Now water some plants or flowers in your garden or house. Talk about some ways God takes care of you.

A PROMISE OF COMFORT

Do you know anyone who feels bad or discouraged today? Jesus promises to comfort us when we feel bad. He will help us in times of trouble.

Praise

Praise Him! Praise Him!

Traditional

Arr. Allan Koppelberger

Praise Him, praise Him, all ye lit-tle chil-dren; God is love, God is love. Praise Him, praise Him, all ye lit-tle chil-dren; God is love, God is love.

Arrangement copyright © 1995 by House of Abraham

40

Prayer

This prayer is based on the Twenty-third Psalm.

Lord,
You are my shepherd; I have everything I need.
You give me rest in green pastures. You lead me to calm
 water.
You give me new strength. For the good of Your Name,
You lead me on paths that are right. Even if I walk through
 a very dark valley, I will not be afraid because You are
 with me.
Your rod and Your walking stick comfort me. You prepare a
 meal for me in front of my enemies.
 You pour oil on my head.
You give me more than I can hold. Surely Your goodness
 and love will be with me all my life.
 And I will live in the house of the Lord forever. Amen.

Promise

"God is our protection and our strength.
He always helps in times of trouble!"

 —*PSALM 46:1*

41

People in the Bible

Jesus told His followers, "Children are very important to God." Then Jesus told a story to show how much God loves His children.

"A man had one hundred sheep. One sheep got lost. The man left the other ninety-nine sheep to search for the lost one. He searched everywhere until he found the lost sheep. The man was very happy."

Jesus said, "The shepherd put the sheep on his shoulders and carried it home. In the same way, your heavenly Father does not want any of His children to be lost."

Later, Jesus told His followers, "I am the Good Shepherd. I know My sheep, and My sheep know Me. The Good Shepherd gives His life for the sheep."

Pleasing God

Help someone feel better by making him or her a *comfort card*. You may want to draw a picture of a lamb and decorate it with cotton balls.

Think of Jesus, the Good Shepherd, as you prepare your card. When you give your friend this card, tell him or her about the Good Shepherd.

I PRAISE GOD FOR HEARING MY PRAYERS

God always answers your prayers! Sometimes the answer is yes. Sometimes the answer is no. Sometimes the answer is wait awhile. He doesn't always give you what you want. But He gives you what you need.

Praise

Lord, Teach a Little Child to Pray

Lord, teach a little child to pray,
And then accept my prayer.
Thou hearest all the words I say
For Thou art everywhere.

A little sparrow cannot fall
Unnoticed, Lord, by Thee,
And though I am so young and small
Thou dost take care of me.

Teach me to do the thing that's right,
And when I sin, forgive,
And make it still my chief delight
To serve Thee while I live.

—JANE TAYLOR

45

Prayer

Please give me what I ask, dear Lord,
If You'd be glad about it.
But if You think it's not for me,
Please help me do without it.

—TRADITIONAL

Promise

"I asked the Lord for help, and he answered me. . . . The Lord sees the
good people. He listens to their prayers. . . .
The Lord hears good people when they cry out to him. He saves them
from all their troubles."

—PSALM 34:4, 15, 17

People in the Bible

Hannah wanted a baby very much. She prayed to God for a son.

She promised he would do God's work all his life. Eli, the priest, saw Hannah praying. "Go in peace," he said. "May God answer your prayer." The Lord God blessed Hannah with a baby boy. She named him Samuel, which means "Asked of God."

Hannah rememberd her promise to God. When Samuel was still a small child, she took him to Eli at the Holy Tent. And Samuel lived with the priest. God was pleased with Hannah because she kept her promise. God blessed Hannah with more children. Hannah became the mother of three more sons and two daughters!

Pleasing God

God hears even the simplest prayer. And He will answer by giving what is best for us. Pretend you are calling God on the telephone. What are some of the things you would like to tell Him? Be sure to tell God you love Him. Thank God for all the good things He has given you. God loves to hear from His children.

HELP ME TO BE KIND AND GOOD

Everyone knows it is better to be good rather than bad. But what does it mean to be good? Being good means to live according to God's Word, the Bible. It means being kind and helping others. It means obeying your parents. Name some other ways you can be good.

Praise

Sing these words to the tune of "Mary Had a Little Lamb."

Help Me to Be Kind and Good

Help me to be kind and good,
To always do the things I should;
Give me wisdom from above,
To share with others God's great love.

Words by Angela Abraham / copyright © 1995 by House of Abraham.

Prayer

All for You, dear God,
Everything I do,
Or think,
Or say,
The whole day long.
Help me to be good.

—AUTHOR UNKNOWN

Promise

"And God gives us the things we ask for. We receive these things
because we obey God's commands, and we do what pleases him."

—1 JOHN 3:22

People in the Bible

Naomi lived in the country of Moab. It was far from her hometown of Bethlehem. Naomi was sad because her husband and sons had died. She decided to move back to Bethlehem. Naomi told her daughter-in-law Ruth, "I am old and poor. You are young and beautiful. Stay here in your own country and remarry."

Naomi was a good woman, and Ruth loved her dearly. Ruth said, "I will stay with you. I will go wherever you go. Your people will be my people. Your God will be my God."

So Ruth left her friends and family to travel with Naomi to the city of Bethlehem. The two widows were very poor. Ruth gathered grain in a nearby field so they would have food to eat.

A rich man named Boaz owned the land. He noticed Ruth working hard in his field. Boaz saw that Ruth was kind and good to her mother-in-law. Boaz married Ruth, and they had a baby boy. Now Naomi and Ruth were happy because God had given them a new family.

53

Pleasing God

Ruth was kind and good to her mother-in-law, Naomi. And God blessed her helpful attitudes and actions.

How can you show kindness to your family members?

Make a *little helper poster*. First, write the days of the week on a posterboard. Now, list several things you can help your parents do around the house, such as keeping your room neat, setting the table, taking out the trash, and putting away toys when you're not playing with them. Keep a chart of the helpful things you remember to do. Ask your parents to help you create a special treat to share with your family at the end of the week (some treat suggestions: ice cream sundaes, brownies, or gelatin). You can review the *little helper poster* as you eat the treat.

HELP ME TO FORGIVE OTHERS

When people treat you mean, how do you treat them in return? How does God feel toward us when we misbehave or act badly? How does God want us to act toward the people who mistreat us?

Praise

Repeat the following rhyme:

> *Thank the Lord every day, for taking all my sins away!*
> *Help me, Lord, every day, to forgive in this same way.*

Clap your hands together after saying each syllable in the rhyme. Now repeat the words, clap your hands, and try marching around the room!

Prayer

This prayer is from Psalm 51:1–2, 9–13.

Dear God,
Be merciful to me because You are loving.
Wash away all my guilt and make me clean again.
Turn Your face from my sins and create in me a pure heart.
Give me back the joy that comes when You save me.
Keep me strong.
Then I will teach Your ways to those who do wrong.
In Jesus' Name, amen.

Promise

"Yes, if you forgive others for the things they do wrong, then your
Father in heaven will also forgive you for the things you do wrong."
                                        —MATTHEW 6:14

People in the Bible

Joseph's brothers were mean to him because they were jealous of him. One day Joseph's brothers grabbed him and threw him in a pit. A group of traders passed by.

"Let's sell Joseph to the traders," the brothers said.

The traders took Joseph to Egypt and sold him as a slave.

Many years passed. Joseph worked very hard, and God blessed him. God helped Joseph become an important leader in Egypt.

When a famine came to the land, Joseph's brothers had to travel to Egypt to buy food. They did not know that Joseph was in charge of giving food to the hungry people. Nor did they know they would have to buy food from Joseph.

Joseph recognized his brothers, but he kept quiet until they visited again.

Finally he said, "Brothers, it is I, Joseph!"

The brothers were surprised and frightened.

"Don't be afraid of me," said Joseph. "God turned into good what you meant to be evil."

Joseph forgave his brothers, even though they had been mean to him. Then Joseph helped his brothers so they would have plenty to eat.

Pleasing God

How would you have treated Joseph's brothers? It isn't always easy to forgive people when they treat us badly. But God wants us to forgive others, just as He forgives us.

Try putting on a *forgiving face*. Draw a big smiley face on one side of a paper plate. Make a list of all the people you need to forgive on the other side of the paper plate.

Ask God to help you forgive each one. Remember that God is pleased when we forgive others.

A PRAYER OF FAITH

What is faith? Faith means being sure of the things we hope for. Believing means knowing that something is real, even if we do not see it.

Praise

Say the words from Psalm 111:1–4 aloud to the Lord:

> *I will thank the Lord with all my heart. . . . The Lord does great things. . . . What He does is glorious and splendid. His goodness continues forever. His miracles are unforgettable. . . .*

Now thank God for some of the great things He has done:

I thank You, Lord, for creating this world.

I thank You, Lord, for making me!

I thank You, Lord, for _____.

61

Prayer

This prayer is based on Mark 11:22–24 and Ephesians 1:18–20.

Lord,
You told us to have faith in God. You said if we believe that what we
ask for will happen, then God will do it.

Help me to have a greater understanding of Your ways. And help me
to realize how great God's power is to those who believe! Amen.

Promise

"'So I tell you to ask for things in prayer. And if you believe that you
have received those things, then they will be yours.'"

—MARK 11:24

People in the Bible

A man named Jairus bowed before Jesus. He begged, "Please heal my little girl. She's dying!"

Jesus went with Jairus, and many people followed. In the crowd was a woman with a blood disease. No one could cure her.

The woman had heard about Jesus' miracles. She believed Jesus could heal her if she could just touch Him through the crowd.

The woman came up behind Jesus as He walked with Jairus. She touched the edge of Jesus' coat. Instantly she was healed.

"Who touched Me?" asked Jesus.

The frightened woman stepped forward. "I did," she said.

Jesus said, "You are healed because you believed."

At the same time, a messenger hurried to Jairus.

"Your daughter is dead!" he cried.

Jesus told Jairus, "Do not be afraid; only believe." At Jairus's house, Jesus held the little girl's hand. He said, "My child, stand up!"

Jairus's daughter stood up. She was well!

Pleasing God

Try making a *prayer box*. Write your prayer requests on strips of paper. Drop them into a shoe box. You may want to decorate the box.

Later, read over your prayers. Have faith that God will answer them. Thank God for all the answered prayers.

A PRAYER IF I POUT OR COMPLAIN

God wants us to sing praises to Him and to say kind words to one another.

He wants us to be happy with what we have, rather than complain about what we don't have.

Praise

O, Be Careful

Traditional   Arr. Allan Kopppelberger

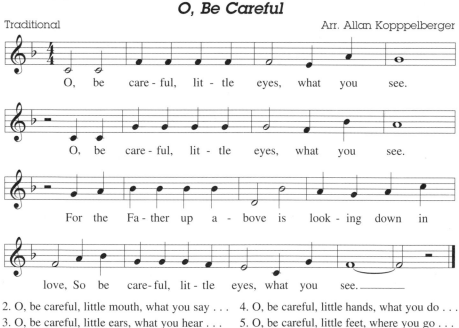

O, be care - ful, lit - tle eyes, what you see.

O, be care - ful, lit - tle eyes, what you see.

For the Fa - ther up a - bove is look - ing down in

love, So be care - ful, lit - tle eyes, what you see. _____

2. O, be careful, little mouth, what you say . . .   4. O, be careful, little hands, what you do . . .
3. O, be careful, little ears, what you hear . . .   5. O, be careful, little feet, where you go . . .

67

Prayer

This prayer is from Psalm 141:3–4.

Lord, help me control my tongue;
Help me be careful about what I say.
Don't let me want to do bad things anywhere I go.
Amen.

Promise

"I will praise you, Lord, with all my heart.
I will tell all the miracles you have done.
I will be happy because of you.
God Most High, I will sing praises to your name."

—Psalm 9:1–2

People in the Bible

After the Israelites left Egypt, they started complaining about all their troubles in the desert. God was not pleased because they had forgotten to be thankful for all the miracles He had done for them.

Then fire burned up part of their camp, and the people cried out to Moses for help.

When Moses prayed, the fire stopped. But God's people didn't stop complaining.

They complained about having no meat to eat. So God sent them quail to eat.

The people had to eat quail every day for a month. And they hated it. They were sorry they had ever grumbled about their food.

Pleasing God

Practice being a "praiser" rather than a "pouter" by singing a song of praise to God. Try adding an instrument while you sing. You can make a drum out of an empty coffee can. You could make a tambourine sound by tapping a pie tin.

Sing the "O, Be Careful," chorus again and add some actions. Cover your eyes when you sing the first verse. Cover your mouth when you sing the second verse, and so on. Cover your ears . . . pray with your hands . . . point to your feet. . . .

A PROMISE WHEN I SHARE

Name some of the wonderful things God has blessed you with. What do you have that you can share with someone? It pleases God when we give to others.

Praise

Give, and It Will Be Given

Angela Abraham

Angela Abraham
Arr. Allan Koppelberger

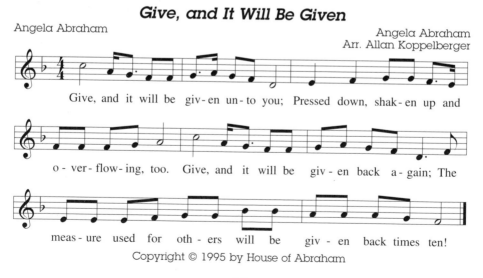

Give, and it will be giv-en un-to you; Pressed down, shak-en up and o - ver - flow - ing, too. Give, and it will be giv - en back a - gain; The meas - ure used for oth - ers will be giv - en back times ten!

Prayer

Dear Lord,
You've blessed me with a lot to share.
So please make me aware
Of the young and the old
Who are needy or cold.
And help me to give what I've got
To those who have not.
Let me show that I care
With what I have to spare.
In Jesus' Name, amen.

Promise

"Give, and you will receive. You will be given much. It will be poured into your hands—more than you can hold. You will be given so much that it will spill into your lap. The way you give to others is the way God will give to you."

—LUKE 6:38

People in the Bible

Elijah was a prophet. God sent Elijah to the home of a poor widow. Elijah asked the woman for a cup of water and a piece of bread.

"All I have is enough flour and oil to make one last meal for my son and me," she said.

"Don't worry," Elijah said. "Trust God to take care of you."

74

"First, bake me a small loaf of bread, then cook for yourself," said Elijah. "The Lord says your jar of flour will never become empty, and the jug will always have oil in it."

The woman did what Elijah told her. The woman shared her little bit of bread, and the Lord blessed her with more. The jar of flour and the jug of oil were never empty.

So Elijah, the widow, and her son had enough food for each day.

Pleasing God

Think of some children who are poor or in need. Maybe you have clothes or toys you can share with them.

Ask your parents if you can create a *care box* of clothes and toys to give these children. Then go with your parents to deliver the donations.

A PRAYER IF I ARGUE OR FIGHT

What do you argue about? How do you feel when you fight? Does it matter to God whether you are right or wrong when you argue?

Praise

Read aloud:

> *Lord, I praise You because You are kind and You show us mercy. You do not become angry quickly. You are full of love. You listen to my prayers for help when I argue with my friends and family. Thank You, Lord, for changing our angry hearts into forgiving hearts of love, just like Yours. Thank You for my friends and family.*

Prayer

"He's wrong! I'm right!"
Push and pull,
Scream and fight.
Lord, I know this isn't pleasing to Your ears.
Please forgive me for yelling,
And dry away these angry tears.
Please help me to get along with others.
Help me to stop fighting with my sisters and my brothers.
In Jesus' Name, amen.

Promise

"Never shout angrily or say things to hurt others. Never do anything evil. Be kind and loving to each other. Forgive each other just as God forgave you in Christ."

—EPHESIANS *4:31–32*

People in the Bible

One day, Jesus overheard His disciples fighting about something.

"What are you arguing about?" Jesus asked His followers.

But the men were ashamed and did not answer. Their argument was about which one of them was the greatest.

Finally, one of Jesus' followers asked Him, "Who is greatest in the kingdom of heaven?"

Jesus called a small child to His side.

Jesus said, "You must change and act like this child, who loves and obeys Me. If you don't do this, you will never enter the kingdom of heaven. The greatest person in the kingdom of heaven is the one who makes himself humble like this child. Do not think children have little value. Children are very important to God. I tell you that they have angels in heaven who are with My Father always!"

Pleasing God

Next time you get into a fight with a friend, try to be the first to make up. Remember to say, "I am sorry. Will you please forgive me?"

You can practice making up right now, by giving someone a great big hug! Then take turns drawing a picture together. Tell a story about the characters each of you adds to the picture.

I PRAISE GOD FOR BLESSINGS

Do you like to hear good things about yourself? So does God! Saying nice things about God is called praise. God loves for us to praise Him.

Praise

Doxology

Thomas Ken (1637–1711)

Louis Bourgeois (1510–c. 1561)
Arr. Allan Koppelberger

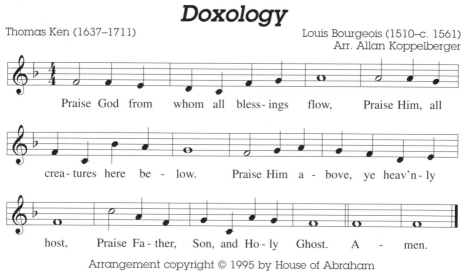

Praise God from whom all bless-ings flow, Praise Him, all crea-tures here be-low. Praise Him a-bove, ye heav'n-ly host, Praise Fa-ther, Son, and Ho-ly Ghost. A - men.

Arrangement copyright © 1995 by House of Abraham

82

Prayer

God Bless

God bless all those that I love,
God bless all those that love me,
God bless all those that love those that I love,
And all those that love those that love me.
                    —NEW ENGLAND SAMPLER

Promise

"The Lord remembers us and will bless us. . . .
The Lord will bless those who fear him,
from the smallest to the greatest."
                    —PSALM 115:12–13

People in the Bible

Many people brought their children to Jesus so He could pray for them. Jesus' followers thought He was too busy teaching to bother with babies. But Jesus said, "Let the little children come to me!" Then He held the children and blessed them.

Pleasing God

List some of the things God has blessed you with. Here are a few things to help you get started:

1. Friends

2. Food

3. Healthy bodies

4. Home

5. _____

Memorize the *God Bless* prayer (page 83) and practice saying it often.

I THANK GOD FOR SUNSHINE OR RAIN

Not every day is bright and sunny. Some days are dark and dreary. But you can thank and praise God, no matter what the weather is outside or how you feel inside.

Praise

Heavenly Sunshine

Henry J. Selley 1859-1942

George H. Cook ? - 1948;
Arr. Allan Koppelberger

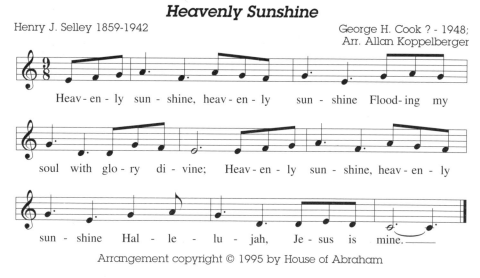

Heav-en-ly sun-shine, heav-en-ly sun-shine Flood-ing my soul with glo-ry di-vine; Heav-en-ly sun-shine, heav-en-ly sun-shine Hal-le-lu-jah, Je-sus is mine.

Prayer

Dear Lord,
In sunshine or rain
You never change,
So I'll praise You the same,
And Your promises claim.
Next time I'm feeling blue,
I know what to do.
I'll lift up Your Name,
And I'll praise You again!
Amen.

Promise

"The heavens tell the glory of God. And the skies announce what his hands have made."

—PSALM 19:1

People in the Bible

God told Noah, "I will flood the earth with water. You will be saved if you obey me."

God told Noah to build a big boat called an ark. Noah did everything God said. Noah built a boat tall and wide. His family and many animals could ride safely inside. Alligators, elephants, monkeys, and bears—pairs of every animal—marched onto the ark. Then God tightly shut the door.

Lightning flashed. Thunder crashed! Rain poured from the sky. It stormed for forty days and nights. The water rose high above the mountain peaks.

Finally, God sent a wind to dry the earth. After many days, the ark touched solid ground. When Noah left the ark, he thanked God for saving his family. God was very pleased. He blessed Noah.

God said, "The earth will never again be destroyed with a flood. A rainbow in the sky will be a sign of My promise to you."

Pleasing God

Remember, Noah trusted God through the flood. He thanked God for saving him and his family.

What do you like to do on a sunny day?

What do you do on a rainy or cloudy day?

Next time it is dark or dreary, have a Noah's ark puppet show! Draw faces on paper lunch bags. Make Noah and some of the animals that were in the ark (lions, bears, giraffes, zebras, cows, lambs, and others). You can decorate your paper puppets with construction paper, felt, yarn, markers, or crayons. When you finish making the puppets, put on a show.

HELP ME TO BE BRAVE

Doesn't it make you feel taller and stronger when your daddy or your mommy picks you up?

God has "strong arms" like that. He promises to lift us up when we ask for His help. He makes us feel brave as we trust Him.

Praise

Sing this chorus to the tune of "Here We Go 'Round the Mulberry Bush."

Our God Is Great and Glorious

Our God is great and glorious.
His ways are all-victorious.
Children come before the King.
And lift our voices, let them sing.
(Repeat)

91

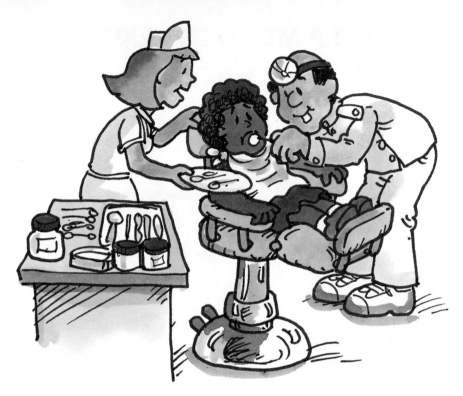

Prayer

This prayer is rewritten from Psalm 18:1–3.

Dear Lord,
I love You. You are my strength. You are my protection. When I need help, I can run to You for safety because You are like a high tower. You give me courage and strength.
Thank You for answering my prayer for help when I call Your Name, amen.

Promise

"'Remember that I commanded you to be strong and brave. So don't be afraid. The Lord your God will be with you everywhere you go.'"
—JOSHUA 1:9

People in the Bible

The Lord told Joshua to cross the Jordan River and lead the children of Israel into the Promised Land.

The Lord said, "Joshua, be strong and brave! Do not be afraid. I will be with you everywhere you go."

Joshua told the people, "Tomorrow, God will do amazing things."

The Israelites prayed. They believed God would perform a miracle for them to enter the Promised Land.

The next day, Joshua told the priests to go to the river and step into the water. The brave priests obeyed Joshua. They carried the Holy Box from the Holy Tent to show that God was with them.

At the moment they stepped into the river, the water stopped flowing! All the people of Israel crossed the Jordan River on dry ground.

Pleasing God

If it's hard for you to be brave in front of other people, try this—sing a solo or recite a poem for your family or a group of people.

Maybe you could try this at church or school.

Ask God to give you courage.

LISTEN TO GOD'S VOICE

How do you think God speaks to you? Would you know His voice if you heard it? God wants to talk to you every day. You are very special to God.

Praise

These Are My Hands

Angela Abraham
Allan Koppelberger

Allan Koppelberger

These are my hands, and with my hands I will praise Him.——

This is my mouth, and with my mouth I will thank Him.——

These are my ears, and with my ears I will lis-ten.——

And with my heart, Lord, I will be faith-ful-ly Yours.——

Prayer

Dear Lord,
Help me to hear Your voice when You speak to me. Please help me to
answer You quickly. Help me to listen and obey Your Word.
In Jesus' Name, amen.

Promise

". . . Speak Lord. I am your servant, and I am listening."
—1 SAMUEL 3:10

97

People in the Bible

One night little Samuel was sleeping in the Holy Tent. A voice called his name. Samuel ran to Eli, the priest and said, "Here I am. What do you want me to do?"

Eli said, "I didn't call you. Go back to bed." Samuel went back to bed. Soon he heard the voice calling him again. Samuel rushed to Eli's side. "I am here. You called me," he said.

"No, Samuel, I didn't call you," Eli said. "Go lie down." Eli realized the Lord was calling Samuel. Eli said, "When you hear the voice again, say, 'Speak, Lord. I am listening.'" So the Lord spoke to Samuel. And Samuel listened to the Lord's voice.

Pleasing God

The main way God will speak to you is through His Word, the Bible. God will also speak to you as you pray. God may speak to you through dreams. Often, you can hear God's voice when the pastor preaches God's Word. Sometimes God speaks to your heart when you praise Him in song. When you hear God speak, it is important to listen and obey.

A PROMISE OF PROTECTION
WHEREVER I GO

Did you know God will protect you everywhere you go?

Ask Him to take care of you and to watch over you. At home or away, at school or at play—God always knows where you are. He has His angels watching over you every day.

Praise

He Leads Me

Joseph H. Gilmore (1834–1918)

William B. Bradbury (1816–1868)
Arr. Allan Koppelberger

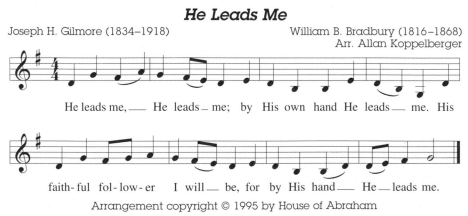

He leads me, ⸺ He leads ⸺ me; by His own hand He leads ⸺ me. His

faith- ful fol- low- er I will ⸺ be, for by His hand ⸺ He ⸺ leads me.

Prayer

Protect me, O Lord;
My boat is so small,
And Your sea is so big.
          —BRETON FISHERMAN'S PRAYER

Promise

"The Lord protects you as the shade protects you from the sun. . . .
The Lord will guard you as you come and go, both now and forever."
          —PSALM 121:5, 8

102

People in the Bible

One day, Jacob and his family were traveling home. Jacob got news that Esau, his angry brother, was nearby.

Esau led an army of fighting men. Jacob feared for his family's safety. Jacob prayed, "Lord, You said You would watch over me! I am afraid Esau will kill us! Please protect us."

Jacob prepared a special gift of many animals for Esau. Jacob thought, *Esau might not fight with me, if he sees this gift*. Jacob prayed again for God's protection.

When Jacob saw Esau, Jacob bowed low before him. Esau was no longer angry. He ran to Jacob and hugged him. Esau was happy to see his brother. God had heard Jacob's prayer. God protected Jacob's family as they traveled.

Pleasing God

Make a *handprint chain.* Trace your hand several times on a sheet of paper. Cut out your handprints. Glue your paper hands side by side on colored construction paper. This picture will remind you that God will hold your hand wherever you go. He promises to protect you with His own hand!

I PRAISE GOD AT CHURCH

Why do you go to church? Who do you learn about at church? What do you do during the church service? Why?

Praise

Joyful, Joyful, We Adore Thee

Henry Van Dyke (1852-1933)

Ludwig Van Beethoven (1770-1827)
Arr. Allan Koppelberger

1. Joy-ful, joy-ful, we a-dore Thee, God of glo-ry, Lord of love;
2. All Thy works with joy sur-round Thee, Earth and heav'n re-flect Thy rays,

Hearts un-fold like flow'rs be-fore Thee, Open-ing to the sun a-bove.
Star and an-gels sing a-round Thee, Cen-ter of un-bro-ken praise;

Melt the clouds of sin and sad-ness; Drive the dark of doubt a-way;
Field and for-est, vale and moun-tain, Bloss'm-ing mea-dow, flash-ing sea,

Giv-er of im-mor-tal glad-ness, Fill us with the light of day!
Chant-ing bird and flow-ing foun-tain, Call us to re-joice in Thee.

106

Prayer

This prayer is based on Psalms 84, 119, 149, and 150.

Lord, the people who go to Your house of prayer are happy. One day in the house of God is better than a thousand days anywhere else! I will praise and worship the Lord in the house of God.

I will sing praises to Your Name. I will praise You for Your power and strength. I will praise You for Your great love. God, I will praise You with all my heart. Your praises will be in my thoughts and on my lips. Lord, help me to follow Your commands and obey Your teaching when I hear Your Word. In Jesus' Name, amen.

Promise

"Happy are the people who live at your Temple. They are always praising you."

—Psalm 84:4

107

People in the Bible

On the Sabbath day, Jesus went to the house of God. He read God's Word to the people.

He said, "The Spirit of the Lord is in Me. God has chosen Me to tell the Good News. He has sent Me to help the sinners and to heal those who are hurting."

Then Jesus began to explain God's Word to the people. All the people praised Jesus. They were amazed at the beautiful words He spoke.

Later, Jesus went to the temple in Jerusalem. He told the people, "My temple will be called a house of prayer." Then Jesus taught in the temple. He healed blind and crippled people there. And the children sang praises to Him: "Hosanna to the Son of David!"

The religious leaders asked Jesus, "Do You hear what the children are saying?"

Jesus answered, "Yes. Haven't you read the Scriptures? It says, 'You have taught children and babies to sing praises.'"

Pleasing God

Jesus went to church on the Sabbath day. He read God's Word. He prayed and worshiped in the house of God. You can follow Jesus' example by going to church to praise and worship God.

Draw a picture of a church building with open doors. This picture will remind you that the church is God's house.

Try this "Here Is the Church" action rhyme:

Here is the church (*fold your hands with your fingers pointing inside toward your palms*).

Here is the steeple (*place index fingers up; touch them together*).

Open the doors (*wiggle your thumbs back and forth*).

And see all the people (*wiggle your fingers inside*).

I PRAISE GOD AT HOME

What does your house look like? How many people live with you there? You may want to draw a picture of your home.

Does Jesus live in your house? Can you worship God at home? How?

Praise

He Is So Precious

Andrea Marceé
Allan Koppelberger

Arr. Allan Koppelberger

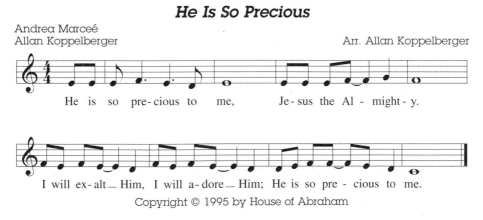

He is so pre-cious to me, Je-sus the Al-might-y.

I will ex-alt— Him, I will a-dore— Him; He is so pre-cious to me.

Copyright © 1995 by House of Abraham

111

Prayer

Lord Jesus,
Help us build our house, we pray,
With faith and trust in God today.
Help us fill this house we share
With joy and peace and loving care.
When the winds and rain assail,
Let our little house prevail.
Please give us shelter from the storm,
And keep the fire in our hearth warm. Amen.

Promise

" . . . You must respect the Lord and serve him fully. . . . You must decide whom you will serve. . . . As for me and my family, we will serve the Lord."

—JOSHUA 24:14–15

People in the Bible

One day Jesus sat on a hillside and taught His followers.

"Everyone who loves and obeys Me is like the wise man who built his house on rock," Jesus said. "The rain poured, the water rose, and the wind beat against the house. But the house did not fall because it was built on rock."

"The person who does not serve or obey Me is like a foolish man who built his house on sand," Jesus said. "Then the storm came, the water rose, and the wind hit the house. The house fell with a big crash."

Pleasing God

Sing this song:

The Wise Man and the Foolish Man

The wise man built his house upon the rock (repeat 3 times),
And the rains came tumbling down.
The rains came down, and the floods came up (repeat 3 times),
And the house on the rock stood firm.

The foolish man built his house upon the sand (repeat 3 times),
And the rains came tumbling down.
The rains came down, and floods came up (repeat 3 times),
And the house on the sand went SMASH!

Add the following actions: 1. Pound one fist in the palm of the other hand (*building a house*). 2. Raise arms, then lower them, wiggling fingers (*rain*). 3. Raise palms upward (*floods*). 4. Touch fingertips together to form a roof (*house on rock stands*) or clap hands together (*house on sand falls*).

Try building your own house out of sand in a sandbox. Pour a cup of water over the house. Watch how quickly the house falls. Now try building a house with rocks or stones. Pour a cup of water over the stone house. Does the house fall?

I PRAISE GOD IN THE MORNING

What do you do first thing in the morning? Do you remember to pray before beginning your day? God wants His children to start each day with praises and prayers to Him.

Praise

This Is My Father's World

Maltbie D. Babcock (1858–1901)

Franklin L. Shepperd (1852–1930)
Arr. Allan Koppelberger

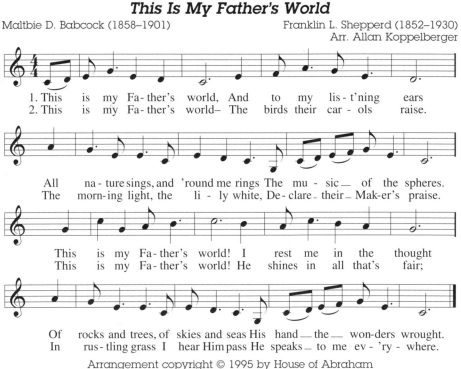

1. This is my Fa-ther's world, And to my lis-t'ning ears
2. This is my Fa-ther's world— The birds their car - ols raise.

All na-ture sings, and 'round me rings The mu - sic of the spheres.
The morn-ing light, the li - ly white, De-clare their Mak-er's praise.

This is my Fa-ther's world! I rest me in the thought
This is my Fa-ther's world! He shines in all that's fair;

Of rocks and trees, of skies and seas His hand the won-ders wrought.
In rus-tling grass I hear Him pass He speaks to me ev - 'ry - where.

Arrangement copyright © 1995 by House of Abraham

Prayer

Good morning, Lord.
You are greatly adored in heaven and earth.
The sun reflects the glory of Your face
And rises to honor Your grace.
The wind whispers Your name,
And the flowers speak of Your fame.
Just as the birds sing Your praise,
I will worship You all of my days!

Promise

". . . I will wake up the dawn. Lord . . . Your love is so great that it is
higher than the skies. Your truth reaches to the clouds. God, you are
supreme over the skies. Let your glory be over all the earth."

—PSALM 108:2–5

117

People in the Bible

Long ago God made the world. The earth was dark. The sky was empty and black. But God's Spirit looked over the world. He had a wonderful plan! When God spoke, the heavens appeared. He blessed the earth with beauty. God shaped the high mountains. He filled the lakes with cool water.

God made the soft grass, fresh fruit, and bright flowers that smell sweet. He told the sun to shine in the day and the stars to twinkle at night. God made fish to splash and swim in the seas. He made birds to sing and fly through the air. Then He filled the earth with animals:

Some that crawl and creep.
Some that jump and leap.

God said, "Let Us make someone to care for My wonderful world!" God molded a man from dirt and breathed life into him. God named the man Adam. Then God formed a woman to help Adam. Her name was Eve. God placed Adam and Eve in a beautiful garden called Eden. In six days, God made every good thing. On the seventh day, He rested from all His work.

Pleasing God

Sing these words to the tune of, "London Bridge Is Falling Down."

> *In the morning I will rise happily with open eyes;*
> *And wherever I may go, I'll see God's glory.*
> *In the morning I will rise happily with open eyes;*
> *I'll see beauty everywhere; Praise the Creator!*
>   —ANGELA ABRAHAM
>
> Copyright © 1995 by House of Abraham

You can use the following actions while singing this song: *Yawn* and *stretch* your arms over your head, *smile*, and *close and open your eyes wide*. Then finish the chorus by *marching around the room*.

A PRAYER AT DAY CARE OR SCHOOL

What are you learning about in school? Have you asked God to help you during school? God promises to give us wisdom and understanding when we pray for His help.

Praise

This action rhyme is based on Proverbs 3.

>Trust in God with all your heart (*cross hands over heart*).
>
>From His Word do not depart (*hold palms upward as though you are holding a Bible*).
>
>Ask God to guide you everyday (*fold hands together in prayer*).
>
>Where you go, and what you say (*drop your hands to sides, march in place, point to mouth*).
>
>Trust in the Lord, today! (*shout and clap three times*).
>
>He will send success your way! (*raise hands heavenward, praise God*).

Prayer

A Prayer at School

S ometimes I wish my friends
C ould see You with them.
H elp my friends know Your ways;
O h, help them to hear Your words today.
O n the playground or during school,
L ord, let me teach them about Your rules!

Promise

"But if any of you needs wisdom, you should ask God for it. God is generous. He enjoys giving to all people, so God will give you wisdom. But when you ask God, you must believe. Do not doubt God. . . ."

—JAMES 1:5–6

123

People in the Bible

In Babylon, King Nebuchadnezzar asked for four young men from Judah to serve in his palace. Daniel and his three friends were chosen. For three years, they studied hard to learn the king's language. And God helped them. God gave these four men wisdom and the ability to learn. Every time the king asked them something important, they showed great understanding. The king discovered that Daniel and his friends were wiser than all the magicians and fortune-tellers in the kingdom.

Pleasing God

Ask God to give you a better understanding of His Word.

Make your own *God Is with Me Book*. Fold several pieces of construction paper in half. Place them together and attach them with a staple. Or punch a hole through the pages and tie them together with a small piece of yarn. Cut out magazine pictures of places to go and things to do. Glue the pictures in your *God Is with Me Book*. Then write the following Bible verse in your book: "Depend on the Lord. Trust him, and he will take care of you," Psalm 37:5.

A PRAYER FOR RECESS AND PLAYTIME

What do you like to do during playtime? Do you remember to think about God and His Word, when you rest?

Praise

Jesus, from Thy Throne on High

> *Jesus, from Thy throne on high,*
> *Far above the bright blue sky,*
> *Look on me with loving eye;*
> *Hear me, Holy Jesus.*
>
> *Be Thou with me every day,*
> *In my work and in my play,*
> *When I learn and when I pray;*
> *Hear me, Holy Jesus.*
>   —THOMAS B. POLLOCK

126

Prayer

Dear God,
Thank You for playtime. Let my life praise You when I am having fun.
Help me not to forget about Your rules when I play. Please help me
remember to share, to be kind and good, to be patient, and to wait
my turn. Help me to show love and to forgive easily. Help me not to
fight. Let me treat others the way I want to be treated. In Jesus'
Name, amen.

Promise

"Happy is the person who doesn't listen to the wicked. He doesn't go
where sinners go. . . . He loves the Lord's teachings. He thinks about
those teachings day and night."

—Psalm *1:1–2*

People in the Bible

God led the people of Israel out of Egypt to the edge of the Red Sea. The Israelites were terrified when they saw the Egyptian king's army racing after them. But God performed a miracle to save His people from the Egyptian army. He caused the water of the Red Sea to separate, and the Israelites were able to cross the sea on dry land. When the Israelites got to the other side, the water came back together. God had saved them from the enemy.

The people of Israel were tired from their frightening journey. But now they could rest safely. Moses' sister, Miriam, took a tambourine in her hand. All the women followed her, playing tambourines and dancing.

They sang: "I will sing to the Lord because He is worthy of great honor. He has thrown the horse and rider into the sea. The Lord gives me strength and makes me sing. He has saved me. He is my God, and I will praise Him."

Pleasing God

Even when you rest or play, remember to praise God. Try making your own play dough (ask a parent to help you):

4 cups flour
2 cups salt
1/4 cup vegetable oil

3 tablespoons cream of tartar
4 cups cold water
(add food coloring if desired)

Mix together the flour, salt, and cream of tartar. Add enough water to make the mixture resemble soft gravel. Finally, add the oil, then mix until thoroughly blended. A few drops of food coloring can be added. Place the mixture in a sauce pan and cook on a stovetop at a low temperature. Stir the mixture constantly until it thickens. Remove the mixture from the heat and allow it to cool. Knead the thickened mixture as though you are making bread dough.

Now, use your imagination and have lots of fun with your own play dough! You can make a variety of shapes (animals, flowers, stars, people, etc.). Think about the things God shaped with His own hands when He created the world!

I THANK GOD BEFORE MEALS

Do you remember to say "please" and "thank you" during mealtime? Do you thank your parents for providing and preparing your meal? It is very important to thank God for your meal!

Praise

For every cup and plateful
God make us truly grateful!
— *TRADITIONAL*

Thank You for the world so sweet,
Thank You for the food we eat,
Thank You for the birds that sing,
Thank You, God, for everything!
— *E. RUTTER LEATHAM (1870–1933)*

Prayer

Dear God,
Thank You for the loved ones at our table.
Please give us good health, and make us able
To praise You for the blessings You bring
At harvest time and through the spring.
For this food now, we humbly bow
To our Father above, who's full of love!
In Jesus' Name, amen.

Promise

"All living things look to you for food. And you give it to them at the right time."

—Psalm 145:15

131

People in the Bible

One day Jesus and His friends went up on a hill and sat down. Many people followed Jesus. Jesus taught the people all day long. After a while, Jesus told His apostles to feed the people.

Philip answered, "It would take a lot of money to buy food for this crowd!"

One little boy had five loaves of bread and two little fish.

He gave them to Andrew, one of Jesus' helpers.

Andrew told Jesus, "This boy will share his meal, but it's not enough." Jesus said, "Tell all the people to sit down for dinner."

Jesus took the bread and fish. He looked up to heaven and thanked God. Then Jesus divided the food and gave it to His followers. They shared it with the hungry people. Everyone had plenty of food to eat. In fact, there were twelve baskets of food left over.

Pleasing God

Remember to be polite and show thanks to your parents, by taking your plate, cup, and eating utensils, to the sink. They will be glad you helped.

Make a *Thanksgiving Placemat* out of construction paper. After decorating your placemat, cover it with clear contact paper. Now, you can use your *Thanksgiving Placemat*, over and over, again!

A BEDTIME PRAYER

Do you have a favorite bedtime prayer?
Would you like to learn a new prayer?
It will be fun!

Praise

Sing these words to the tune of "Are You Sleeping?"

I Will Trust Him

I will trust Him, I will trust Him.
I won't fear, I won't fear.
I have the faith to close my eyes,
And rest in peace throughout the night.
'Cause I know my God is near.
'Cause I know my God is here!

—ANGELA ABRAHAM

Prayer

Good-Night Prayer

Father, unto Thee I pray,
Thou hast guarded me all day;
Safe I am while in Thy sight,
Safely let me sleep tonight.

Bless my friends, the whole world bless;
Help me to learn helpfulness;
Keep me ever in Thy sight;
So to all I say good-night.
                    —HENRY JOHNSTONE

Promise

"The Lord listens when I pray to him. I go to bed and sleep in peace.
Lord, only you keep me safe."

                    —PSALM 4:3, 8

People in the Bible

Jacob set out on a long journey. He was going to live in the land where his grandfather lived.

He had to stop when the sun set. He spent the night in a lonely place. He slept on the ground. And he used a stone for a pillow.

In a dream, Jacob saw angels climbing up and down a ladder to heaven. God was standing above the ladder.

He said, "I will protect you everywhere you go. I will not leave you."

When Jacob woke up, he said, "Surely the Lord is in this place."

Before Jacob continued his journey, he made a promise. "I will give God one-tenth of all He gives me."

138

Pleasing God

Try singing "I Will Trust Him" before you go to bed. Sing this song to the tune "Are You Sleeping?" Have fun using the following motions.

I (*point to self*) will trust Him (*point heavenward. Repeat*).

I (*point to self*) won't fear (*shake head, "No." Repeat*).

I (*point to self*) have the faith to close my eyes (*close eyes*),

And rest in peace throughout the night (*lean hands against cheek, as though you are sleeping. Keep your eyes closed*).

'Cause I know my God is near (*raise hands heavenward*).

'Cause I know my God is here (*fold hands over your heart*)!

A PROMISE DURING DOCTOR VISITS

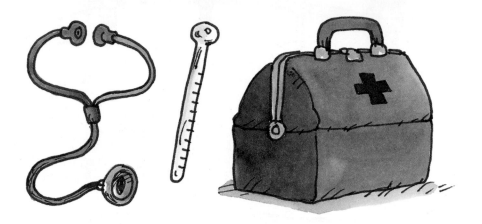

Did you know God goes with you when you go to the doctor's office? It will make you feel better to remember that the same God who made your body can heal your body!

Praise

Lift up your hands and praise the Lord as you read aloud these words from Psalm 139.

> *"Lord . . . I praise you because you made me in an amazing and wonderful way. What You have done is wonderful. . . . You saw my bones being formed as I took shape in my mother's body. . . . You saw my body as it was formed. All the days planned for me were written in your book before I was one day old."*

Now clap your hands together and thank God for making you special.

Prayer

This prayer is based on Psalm 139.

Dear Lord,
You know when I sit down and when I get up. You know my thoughts
before I think them. Even before I say a word, You already know what I
am going to say. You know where I go and everything I do. Your
knowledge is amazing to me! If I whisper a prayer quietly, You hear
me. If I think something, You hear it. If I pray in my thoughts without
any words, You still hear me. Please let my thoughts and words always
please You. And be with me today, Lord Jesus. Amen.

Promise

"Do not worry about anything. But pray and ask God for everything
you need. And when you pray always give thanks. And God's peace
will keep your hearts and minds in Christ Jesus. . . . Think about the
things that are good and worthy of praise. . . . And the God who gives
peace will be with you."

—PHILIPPIANS 4:6–9

People in the Bible

Hezekiah became sick with a deadly disease. Isaiah the prophet said, "The Lord says you will not get better."

Hezekiah was afraid. He cried to the Lord, "God, please be with me. Lord, remember how I've always tried to obey You." Then Hezekiah asked God to heal him. Hezekiah prayed that God would bless him with a long life.

God gave Isaiah a message for Hezekiah. Isaiah said, "The Lord says you will be healed. God will add many years to your life."

Isaiah told Hezekiah to put medicine on his body. Then Isaiah prayed for Hezekiah. And the Lord healed Hezekiah.

Pleasing God

Thank God for creating you by making a book about yourself.

Join several pieces of paper together with staples or punch holes in the papers and tie them together with yarn. Write "I Am a Child of God" on the cover of your book. Find a photograph of yourself and glue it to the cover. On the second page, write your name, address, and phone number. On the third page, write your birth date, your eye color, and your hair color. Put your fingerprints on the fourth page. Rub your fingers in paint, then press your fingers to the paper. You may want to add a picture of your family to remind you of the people who love you. Draw a picture of Jesus in your book to remind you of God's love. This book will remind you that God made you special and unique!

I PRAISE GOD ON THE MOUNTAINS OR AT THE BEACH

Can you praise God quietly? How?

Do you pray to God when you are with other people?

Praise

This praise is based on Psalm 95:2–7.

While you read it, think about how great the Lord is. Thank God quietly in your thoughts.

> *"Let's come to God with thanksgiving. The Lord is great. He is King over all gods. The deepest places on earth are His. And the highest mountains belong to Him. The sea is His because He made it. He created the land with His own hands. Come, let us bow down and worship Him. Let's kneel before the Lord who made us. He is our God. And we are the people He takes care of."*

145

Prayer

Lord, in the Scriptures You have said, "Be quiet and know that I am God." Please help me to be still before You. I want to listen to Your voice and trust Your Word. Let me quiet myself in Your presence. As I think about You, please speak to my heart.

Promise

"God says, 'Be quiet and know that I am God. I will be supreme over all the nations. I will be supreme in the earth.'"

—PSALM 46:10

People in the Bible

One day a crowd of people followed Jesus to Lake Galilee. They wanted to hear the Word of God.

Jesus saw two boats near the shore. The boats belonged to a group of fishermen—Peter, Andrew, James, and John. Jesus got into Peter's boat and taught the people on the shore.

Later, Jesus told Peter, "Put your nets in the deep water, and you will catch fish."

Peter said, "Master, we tried all night, and we didn't catch any fish."

Peter and the other fishermen obeyed Jesus anyway.

They caught so many fish that the nets began to break. The fishermen were amazed at the miracle. Peter bowed before Jesus.

Jesus said, "From now on you will fish for men." The fishermen left their boats on the shore and followed Jesus everywhere.

Pleasing God

You can finish this thanksgiving psalm (Psalm 136:1, 5–6) from your own heart. Try playing charades with a friend or parent. Let someone guess what you are thankful for while you act out the answers!

"Give thanks to the Lord because he is good.
His love continues forever. . . .
With his wisdom he made the skies.
His love continues forever.
God spread out the earth on the seas.
His love continues forever. . . ."

I will give thanks to the Lord for _____.
His love continues forever.
I will praise God at all times because _____.
His love continues forever.
I will praise God when I am _____.
His love continues forever.
I will praise God when I go _____.
His love continues forever.

I PRAISE GOD FOR GIVING HIS WORD

Do you read God's Word every day? Through His Word, God teaches us how to live right. God speaks to our hearts when we read His Word. We know God better when we learn His Word.

Praise

Sing or say the words to the following traditional Bible school song:

The B-I-B-L-E

The B-I-B-L-E,
Yes, that's the book for me,
I stand upon the Word of God,
The B-I-B-L-E.

Prayer

This prayer is based on Psalm 119:33–35, 105, 171–172.

Your word is like a lamp for my feet and a light for my way.
Let me praise You and sing about Your promises. Teach me Your
commands. Then I will obey Your Word forever. Help me understand
Your teaching, so I can obey Your rules with all my heart.
In Jesus' Name, amen.

Promise

"The Lord's teachings are perfect. They give new strength. The Lord's
rules can be trusted. They make plain people wise. The Lord's orders
are right. They make people happy. . . . Keeping them brings great
reward."

—Psalm 19:7–8, 11

People in the Bible

When the Israelites reached Mount Sinai, God called Moses to the mountaintop. God said, "I am the Lord your God. I brought you out of slavery in Egypt."

Then God gave ten rules to help His people live right. He wrote these commandments on stone tablets.

- I am the only, one true God. Love and worship Me.

- Do not worship or serve any other god.

- Do not curse or swear using God's name.

- Rest on the Sabbath day; keep it holy.

- Honor your father and mother.
- Do not kill people.
- Husbands and wives be faithful to each other.
- Do not steal.
- Do not lie.
- Do not wish for things that belong to someone else.

God told Moses, "I have written My rules. Now you can teach them to the people."

Pleasing God

Every day, remember to read God's Word. Then allow God time to speak to your heart through His Word.

Shout the following "Bible Cheer":

"Give me a B!" (Echo B.) "Give me an I!" (Echo I.)

"Give me a B!" (Echo B.) "Give me an L!" (Echo L.)

"Give me an E!" (Echo E.)

"What does it spell?" (Bible!)

"Say it again, louder." (BIBLE!)

"Who gave you the Word?" (God did!)

"And who should you praise?" (The Lord!)

"Now, give God a loud clap offering of praise!" (Clap hands together.)

Try making *Ten Commandments Tablets* out of cardboard. Write down the ten rules on the cardboard with a marker. Place your tablets on your dresser. Each morning, you can memorize a new commandment. After ten days, recite all ten commandments for your parents. Ask them to help you decide on a special reward for learning God's Word!

I THANK GOD FOR SENDING HIS SON

Have you asked Jesus to be your Savior?

Pray for Jesus to come into your heart.

Praise God for sending His Son to save you.

Praise

Down in My Heart

I have the joy, joy, joy, joy down in my heart, (where?)
down in my heart, (where?) down in my heart.
I have the joy, joy, joy joy down in my heart, (where?)
down in my heart to stay.
And I'm so happy, so very happy,
I have the love of Jesus in my heart.
And I'm so happy, so very happy,
I have the love of Jesus in my heart.

Add the following actions:
1. Clap four times *(joy)*.
2. Cross hands over your heart *(heart)*.
3. Cup hands and SHOUT *(where?)*.
4. Lift hands heavenward *(happy)*.

155

Prayer

Jesus, Friend of Little Children

Jesus, friend of little children,
Be a friend to me
Take my hand and ever keep me
Close to Thee.
Teach me how to grow in goodness,
Daily as I grow:
Thou hast been a child, and surely
Thou dost know.
Never leave me, nor forsake me;
Ever be my friend;
For I need Thee, from life's dawning
To its end.

—WALTER J. MATHAMS (1853–1931)

Promise

"... My soul praises the Lord; my heart is happy because God is my Savior.... God has done what he promised...."

—LUKE 1:46–47, 55

People in the Bible

One day God sent an angel to Mary. The angel said,
"Don't be afraid. God has chosen you to be the mother of
Jesus. This Holy Child will be the King that God promised.
And He will be called the Son of God."

Next, an angel appeared to Joseph in a dream. "Don't be
afraid to take Mary as your wife. The baby inside her is
from the Holy Spirit," the angel said. "You will call Him
Jesus, which means, The Lord Saves."

So Joseph and Mary were married.

The emperor said all the people must go to their birthplaces to list their names and to pay taxes. Joseph and Mary traveled many miles to Bethlehem, their hometown.

Mary was very tired, but there was no place to rest. Bethlehem was crowded with people. Mary and Joseph had to spend the night in a stable.

During the night, Mary's baby was born. She wrapped Him in warm clothes and made a cozy bed for Him in a feedbox.

Some shepherds were watching their sheep in a nearby field. Suddenly an angel appeared. The shepherds were frightened.

The angel said, "Don't be afraid. I am bringing you good news. Tonight your Savior was born in Bethlehem. He is Christ the Lord."

Then a choir of angels sang, "Glory to God in heaven."

Pleasing God

What can I give Him,
Poor as I am?
If I were a shepherd,
I would bring Him a lamb.
If I were a wise man,
I would do my part.
But what can I give Him?
Give Him my heart.

— CHRISTINA G. ROSSETTI (1830–1894)

Remember to thank God for sending His Son. At Christmas time try making dough ornaments that show God's love.

2 cups flour	1 cup water
1 cup salt	1 teaspoon alum

Mix the dry ingredients together. Add water to the dry mix. Knead the dough for eight to ten minutes. Form the dough into desired shapes (stars, angels, hearts, lambs, etc.). Poke a hole in the top of the ornament with a toothpick.

Bake on a cookie sheet in an oven at 200 degrees for two hours. (Or, if time allows, the finished craft can air dry, uncovered for several days.) Almost any kind of paint can be used to decorate the dried dough ornaments (oil, tempra, spray paint). Lace ribbon through the hole at the top of the finished ornament. Now it is ready to hang on a Christmas tree.

I THANK GOD FOR THE HOLY SPIRIT

Who is the Holy Spirit?

He is Jesus' presence on earth.

The Holy Spirit helps us learn about Jesus. He helps us pray. He causes us to want to praise the Lord more. The Holy Spirit always points us to Jesus!

Praise

Can't Stop Talkin' 'bout Jesus

Words by Ken and Angela Abraham

Music by Tink Abraham
Arr. by Allan Koppelberger

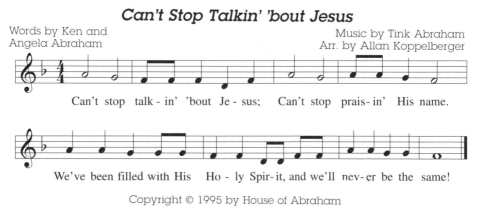

Can't stop talk-in' 'bout Je-sus; Can't stop prais-in' His name.

We've been filled with His Ho-ly Spir-it, and we'll nev-er be the same!

Prayer

Dear Jesus,
Please forgive me when I forget to obey You. Thank You for giving Your
life to save me. Please fill me with Your Holy Spirit so You can help me
know how to live right. Let me be a powerful witness for You. I want
everyone to hear about the Good News. Jesus, I want everyone to know
You came to bring new life and hope to the world. Amen.

Promise

"' . . . The Father has made you a promise. . . . The Holy Spirit will
come to you. Then you will receive power. You will be my witnesses . . .
in every part of the world.'"

—ACTS 1:4, 8

163

People in the Bible

Each day Jesus' followers met together to pray. The believers were waiting for the promise from God. During this time, the believers gathered to celebrate Pentecost. This was the Jewish Harvest Festival. Suddenly a noise came from heaven. It sounded like a strong wind blowing, and it filled the whole house. It looked as though a tongue of fire rested on the head of each believer.

All the believers were filled with the Holy Spirit, and they began to speak in different languages.

Jewish people from every country were in Jerusalem for Pentecost. They were surprised. "How can this be?" they said. "We hear these believers speaking in our own languages about the great things God has done!"

Peter stood up and boldly told the people the good news about Jesus. "Be baptized in the name of Jesus," Peter said. "Let Jesus forgive you and save you from sin! Then you will receive the Holy Spirit too!" The people who believed what Peter said were baptized. About three thousand people were added to the the number of believers that day.

Pleasing God

Make your own *Spirit banner*. Draw a beautiful rainbow
with markers on poster board. Sprinkle and glue glitter to
your rainbow. This will remind you of all God's beautiful
promises. Now draw a white dove near the rainbow.
Decorate the dove with felt or feathers. This will remind you
about God's promise to give His Holy Spirit to those who
follow Jesus.

I THANK GOD FOR ANGELS

God made angels to praise Him in heaven and to watch over His children on earth. Most of the time, we cannot see angels. But we know that God sends angels to help us. They go where God sends them. They do what God tells them to do. They come into our homes, churches, and schools. And one even protected Daniel in a lions' pit!

Praise

All Night, All Day

Spiritual   Arr. Allan Koppelberger

All night, all day, an-gels watch-in' o-ver me, my Lord.

All night, all day, an-gels watch-in' o-ver me.

Arrangement copyright © 1995 by House of Abraham

167

Prayer

Thank You, Father above, for sending angels to guard me with love. It helps me to know that wherever I go and whatever I do, Your angels will follow and watch me there, too!
Amen.

Promise

"He has put his angels in charge of you.
They will watch over you wherever you go."

—PSALM 91:11

168

People in the Bible

The Bible tells about a brave man named Daniel.

Daniel dared to pray to God even when King Darius made a law that said no one could pray to any god but him. Anyone who disobeyed this law was to be thrown into a lions' pit. Daniel heard about the law. But it did not stop him from praying to the Lord God.

Some men told King Darius about Daniel's prayers.

Poor Daniel was thrown into the lions' pit. The hungry
lions came running to eat Daniel. But they could not even
open their mouths. God sent an angel to keep them away
from Daniel. The next morning, King Darius hurried to the
lions' pit. He called, "Daniel, has the God you worship been
able to save you?"

"Yes," Daniel answered. "I am safe. God sent an angel to
close the lions' mouths."

Pleasing God

Why do you think Daniel refused to stop praying?

Do you pray each day?

Ask your parents to help you remember to pray.

You may want to draw an angel. What do you think your guardian angel might look like? Hang your picture on the refrigerator to help remind you that God's angels are watching over you.

BLESS MY FAMILY

Did you know that God will bless your family when you ask Him?

Praise

The words of the following song can be sung to the tune, "Twinkle, Twinkle, Little Star."

Bless My Little Family

Bless my little family dear;
Keep us safe year after year.
Help us shower those we love;
With lots of kisses, lots of hugs.
Bless my little family dear;
Keep us safe year after year.

Fill the loving home we share
With understanding, tender care.
Keep us faithful every day
In what we do and what we say.
Fill the loving home we share
With understanding, tender care.

Prayer

Dear Lord,
Bless our home with happiness year after year;
And when sadness comes, quickly dry away our tears.
Protect our home with Your great love,
Watching over the ones I love;
For there's no place I'd rather be,
than with my precious family.
Amen.

Promise

"The father of a good child is very happy.
The person who has a wise son is glad because of him. Make your
father and mother happy. Give your mother a reason to be glad."

—PROVERBS *23:24–25*

173

People in the Bible

Abram worshiped God. His neighbors prayed to false gods.

God told Abram, "Leave this country. Go to a new land, and I will bless you."

Abram obeyed God. He packed all his things and moved.

Then God appeared to Abram and said, "I will give to your family all the land you see."

Abram thanked God.

One night God spoke to Abram in a vision. "Can you count the stars at night? I will bless you with so many children, you will not be able to count them."

Abram believed God.

Later, God changed Abram's name to Abraham. Again God said, "You will be father of many."

Abraham was ninety-nine years old. God said, "Your wife, Sarah, will have a son."

Abraham said, "Sarah and I are too old to have children."

"Is anything too hard for the Lord?" said God. And the Lord remembered His promise.

Isaac was the son born to Sarah and Abraham. Isaac means "laughter."

Pleasing God

"This Is My Family" Finger Play

"Here is my momma, who cares for us all"
(*hold up one index finger*).

"Here is my daddy, who stands proud and tall"
(*hold up middle finger and index finger*).

"Here is my big (or little) brother (or sister)"
(*hold up ring finger, middle, and index fingers*).

"He helps *me* when I fall"
(*hold up little finger with all the other fingers*).

"This is my puppy dog" (*hold out thumb*).

"He wags his tail, when I call" (*wiggle thumb back and forth*).

177

PRAISE GOD FOR MY FRIENDS

What are the names of your friends?

Do you enjoy doing nice things for your friends?

What is the best thing you can do to help your friends?

Praise

With a friend, do the following clapping routine. As you say each "thank you," praise God for all the friends He has given you.

THANK *(Clap both hands together with your friend's hands.)*

YOU,   *(Clap your own hands together.)*

LORD, *(Clap both your knees with your hands.)*

FOR   *(Clap your own hands together again.)*

ALL   *(Clap opposite hands with your friend.)*

MY   *(Clap your own hands together again.)*

FRIENDS.   *(Clap opposite hands with your friend.)*

Thank You, Lord for every one. *(Repeat clapping routine)*

Thank You, Lord for my friend _ _____.

(Repeat clapping routine as you name a friend.)

178

Prayer

This is a prayer from Philippians 1:9–11.

A Friend's Prayer

This is my prayer for you:
That your love will grow more and more;
That you will see the difference between good and bad
    and chose the good;
That you will do many good things with the help of Christ
    to bring glory and praise to God.
In Jesus' Name, amen.

Promise

"I thank God every time I remember you.
And I always pray for all of you with joy."
                                        —*Philippians 1:3–4*

179

People in the Bible

Jesus went to a wedding with His mother, Mary, and some friends.

There wasn't enough wine for the feast. And the bridegroom was upset.

Mary asked Jesus to help.

Jesus said, "Why come to Me?"

But Mary trusted Jesus to do the right thing. She told the servants, "Do whatever Jesus tells you to do."

Jesus told the servants to fill six big jars with water.

When the bridegroom tasted the water, he was surprised. The water had become wine.

Jesus performed this miracle to help His friends.

Pleasing God

Ask your parents if you could make a *prayer album,* with pictures of friends you'd like to pray for. Fold a large piece of construction paper in half to make a prayer book. Fasten the pictures to the construction paper with a stapler or tape. You may want to decorate the cover of your *prayer album* with a photo or drawing. Remember to pray for the friends in your *prayer album* each day.

HELP MY NEIGHBORS

Who are your neighbors? Are the people who live in other lands or countries your neighbors?

Do you pray for the people who live in other countries? Remember to pray for the missionaries and preachers who teach people in other countries about Jesus.

Praise

This Is My Commandment

Traditional
(John 15:12)

Arr. by Allan Koppelberger

This is My com-mand-ment that you love one an-oth-er, that your

joy may be full. This is My com-mand-ment that you

love one an-oth-er, that your joy may be full. That your

joy may be full, that your joy may be full; This is My com -

mand-ment, that you love one an-oth-er, That your joy may be full.

Arrangement copyright © 1995 by House of Abraham

183

Prayer

Lord, I love You with all my heart and soul. Please help me to love my neighbors. Help me to treat them the same way I would like to be treated. Help me remember that my neighbors are everywhere. . . . the people in the house next door. . . . the people who live in other lands or countries. Help me to please You, Lord, by showing love to others. In Jesus' Name, amen.

Promise

"'Love the Lord your God. Love him with all your heart, all your soul, all your strength, and all your mind.' Also, 'You must love your neighbor as you love yourself. . . . Do this and you will have life forever.'"

—LUKE 10:27–28

People in the Bible

One day a Jewish lawyer asked Jesus, "What must I do to go to heaven?"

"What does God's law say?" asked Jesus.

"Love the Lord with all your heart and your neighbor as yourself," he answered.

"You are right," said Jesus.

"But who is my neighbor?" asked the lawyer.

Jesus told him a story. "Once a traveler was attacked by robbers. They beat him and left him to die in a ditch. Then a priest passed by. But when he saw the injured man, he walked by on the other side of the road."

"Next a temple worker hurried by. He didn't stop to help either. Finally, a foreigner saw the poor man. He bandaged the man's wounds. Then he lifted the man out of the ditch and took him to a safe place."

Jesus asked the lawyer, "Which man was a good neighbor to the hurting stranger?"

"The man who helped him," said the lawyer.

Jesus said, "Go and do the same thing. Take care of the hurting people around you."

Pleasing God

Love God with All Your Soul and Strength

Love God with all your soul and strength
With all your heart and mind.
And love your neighbor as yourself:
Be faithful, just and kind.
Deal with another as you'd have
Another deal with you.
What you're unwilling to receive,
Be sure you never do.
—ISAAC WATTS (1674–1748)

Choose someone in your neighborhood and pray for them every night for one week. To let them know you care, tell them you prayed for them.

BLESS MY TEACHERS

How does God teach His children?

Do you think of your grandparents, parents, sisters, brothers, and friends as your teachers? List some of your other teachers: Sunday school teacher, preacher, schoolteacher, piano instructor, soccer coach, and others.

Is there anything you can teach? How?

Praise

Do any of your teachers remind you of God? How?

Read the words of Proverbs 1. Can you think of people who do what this scripture says? It describes those who teach wisdom and give understanding. They "teach you what is honest and fair and right." They "teach the ability to think to those with little knowledge." They give "good sense to the young."

Praise and thank God for all your teachers. List them by name:

Lord, I thank You for_____ who teaches me_____. Please bless_____ for helping me learn about_____.

Prayer

You can say the following prayers from Scripture for your teachers:

Lord, give_____the right words to teach others the good news about Jesus, without fear. (Ephesians 6:19)
Lord, I pray that_____ will have great wisdom and understanding about You. (Colossians 1:9)
Lord, help_____ live the kind of life that pleases You in every way. (Colossians 1:10)
And Lord, please help me to teach_____about_____.

Promise

"Whoever spends time with wise people will become wise. . . ."
                                        —PROVERBS *13:20*

People in the Bible

Jesus used many stories to teach His followers about God's kingdom.

"A farmer went out to plant seeds," Jesus said.

"As he scattered the seeds, some fell beside the road. The birds came and ate them all."

He said, "Some seeds fell on rocky ground. When they grew, the hot sun burned those little plants because they had short roots. Other seeds fell among weeds that would later choke the growing plants. But the seeds that fell on good soil grew into strong, healthy plants."

The people asked, "What does this story mean?"

Jesus explained, "The seed is the Word of God. Some people hear His Word; then Satan steals it from them. Other people listen but give up easily when problems come. Others let worries and love of money crowd God from their hearts."

Jesus said, "The people who learn about God's teaching and understand it are like the seeds planted on good soil. They grow into beautiful 'plants.' Then they teach others about the good news of Jesus."

Pleasing God

Make a special gift for a favorite teacher. Try making a *Popsicle-stick photo frame.* Glue four Popsicle sticks together to form a square. Decorate the frame by gluing seeds or dry pasta pieces to it. Paint the seeds or dry noodles a bright color. Now tape a photograph of you and your favorite teacher to the frame. Give the framed photograph to your teacher. Thank your teacher for teaching you. Tell him or her how much you appreciate his or her patience while you are learning.

I PRAISE GOD FOR PETS

Do you have a pet? If you could create your own pet, what would it look like? What would you name it? Praise God for filling the world with so many beautiful and different animals.

Praise

All Things Bright and Beautiful

All things bright and beautiful,
All creatures great and small,
All things wise and wonderful,
The Lord God made them all.

He gave us eyes to see them,
And lips that we might tell,
How great is God Almighty,
Who has made all things well.

—CECIL FRANCES ALEXANDER (1818–1895)

193

Prayer

Dear Father,
Hear and bless
Thy beasts and singing birds.
And guard with tenderness
Small things that have no words.
                    —UNKNOWN

Promise

"God says, 'My people listen to me. . . . I am God, your God. . . . Every
animal of the forest is already mine. The cattle on a thousand hills are
mine. I know every bird on the mountains. Every living thing in the
field is mine. . . . The earth and everything on it are mine."
                    —PSALM 50:7,10–12

People in the Bible

King Balak was afraid of Israel. He wanted to drive the Israelites back into the desert. He sent a message to the prophet Balaam: "Come and curse Israel. I will give you a great reward."

But God warned Balaam. "Do not curse Israel," He said. "I have already blessed them."

God told Balaam, "Go to Balak. But only do what I tell you." Balaam saddled his donkey and traveled toward Balak's country. God knew Balaam really wanted the reward from Balak.

God sent an angel with a sword to stop Balaam. Balaam's donkey saw the angel but Balaam didn't. The donkey ran off the road. Balaam hit him and forced him back onto the road. The Lord made Balaam's donkey talk.

"Why are you hitting me?" asked the donkey.

Balaam said, "You're making me look like a fool!"

"Have I ever done this before?" said the donkey.

Suddenly Balaam saw the angel and fell to the ground. "I have sinned," said Balaam. "I did not see you blocking the road."

So Balaam blessed Israel instead of cursing them. And God used Balaam's donkey to save Balaam's life.

Pleasing God

It is important to take good care of the animals God placed in the world. If you have a pet, remember to care for it with love. If you don't have a real animal, make a pretend "pet" out of an oatmeal box. What kind of pet would you like? A rabbit? A dog? A cat?

Decorate the box the way you want your pet to look. Color the box with crayons, paint, or markers. Glue buttons or dry macaroni to the box for your pet's eyes. Next, make ears and a mouth for your pet from felt or contruction paper. Add a tail with cotton balls or yarn. Now, name your new pet! Think about how much God must enjoy creating all the different animals in the world.

A PROMISE WHEN MY FRIENDS NEED HELP

Think of some of the ways your friends may be hurting. Maybe someone is in the hospital. Someone else may have a family member or pet that died. Others may feel sad because his or her parents are divorced. What can you do to help your friends when they are hurting? Do you remember to pray for your friends when they need help?

Praise

Evening Hymn

I hear no voice, I feel no touch,
I see no glory bright;
But yet I know that God is near,
In darkness as in light.

He watches ever by my side,
And hears my whispered prayer:
The Father for His little child
Both night and day doth care.
　　　　　　　—Anonymous

Prayer

You can pray the following prayers from Scripture for your friends:

Lord, I pray that You will help _____ with Your great power. Please be with _____ so he/she will not give up when sad or bad things happen. (Colossians 1:11)

Lord, You want all people to be saved. You want everyone to know the truth. Please help me to be able to tell _____ about You. I pray that _____ will come to know You as his/her Savior. (1 Timothy 2:4)

Promise

"He heals the brokenhearted. He bandages their wounds."
—Psalm *147:3*

People in the Bible

Jesus often stayed at the home of Mary, Martha, and Lazarus. Jesus enjoyed visiting with His friends. One day the sisters sent a message to Jesus: "Lazarus is very sick!"

Jesus said to His followers, "This sickness is so people can see the power of God and praise Him."

Jesus loved Lazarus, but it was two days before He went to see His friend.

When Jesus got there, Lazarus had died and was buried in a cave.

Martha said, "Lord, if You had been here, my brother wouldn't have died!"

Jesus replied, "He who believes in Me will have life even if he dies." Mary fell at Jesus' feet and cried. Jesus felt very sad. Jesus cried with his friends.

Jesus prayed. Then He said, "Lazarus, come out!" Lazarus walked out of the cave. He was alive again! Many people saw Jesus raise Lazarus from the dead. From then on, they believed in Jesus.

Pleasing God

Jesus felt sad when He heard the bad news about Lazarus. Jesus cried with His friends Mary and Martha and comforted them in their sorrow. Then He gave Lazarus the gift of life.

Be sure to tell your friends that Jesus loves them and wants to help them. And don't forget to show your friends that you love them, too. Let them know that you care about them when they are having problems.

First, you can comfort your friends with kind words of encouragement. Tell them that no problem is too big for Jesus to handle. Next, you can try to help them by giving them something they may need, such as food, clothes, or money. The most important thing you can do when your friends are hurting is to keep on being their friend!

"The Lord will keep his promises. With love he takes care of all he has made."

—PSALM 145:13

INDEX

Bible Heroes

Songs of Praise

"Speak to each other with psalms, hymns, and spiritual songs. Sing and make music in your hearts to the Lord."
—EPHESIANS 5:19

Hymns

Doxology 82
He Leads Me 101
Joyful, Joyful, We Adore Thee ...106
This Is My Father's World..........116

Choruses

All Night, All Day 167
The B–I–B–L–E............................150
Bless My Little Family 172
Can't Stop Talkin' 'bout Jesus 162
Cast Your Cares 36
Down in My Heart......................155
Give, and It Will Be Given 72
God's Love Is Amazing...............1
He Is So Precious.........................111
Heavenly Sunshine.....................86
Help Me to Be Kind and Good ...50

If You're Angry/Happy 21
I Will Trust Him 135
In the Morning I Will Rise.................121
O, Be Careful.......................................67
Our God Is Great and Glorious 91
Praise God When I Am Happy...........6
Praise Him! Praise Him!......................40
The Wise Man and the Foolish Man ...115
These Are My Hands...........................96
This Is My Commandment.................183
Whisper a Prayer 26

Scriptures

Acts 1:4, 8 163
Acts 2:1–47.........................164, 165
Acts 9:36–43.......................33, 34
2 Chronicles 32:24 142
Colossians 1:9 189
Colossians 1:10 189
Colossians 1:11 199
Daniel 1 124
Daniel 6 ....169, 170
Deuteronomy 31:1–8.........93, 94
Ephesians 1:18–20.............62
Ephesians 4:31, 32.............22, 78
Ephesians 5:1, 2.................22
Ephesians 6:19 189

Esther.................................28, 29
Exodus 14–15:21..............128
Exodus 19–24....................152, 153
Exodus 33, 34....................152, 153
Genesis 1–2 118–120
Genesis 4 ....23, 24
Genesis 6–9:17 ....88, 89
Genesis 12; 13; 15;
    17; 18; 21:1–7 174–176
Genesis 27:41–46; 28........137, 138
Genesis 32–33:11 ....103, 104
Genesis 37; 39–50 57–59
Hebrews 13:5–6 17
Isaiah 38 142

Subject